THE CASE FOR SMALL BUSINESS

PAUL-PHILIP

iUniverse LLC
Bloomington

The Case for Small Business

iUniverse books may be ordered through booksellers or by contacting:

iUniverse LLC
1663 Liberty Drive
Bloomington, IN 47403
www.iuniverse.com
1-800-Authors (1-800-288-4677)

Because of the dynamic nature of the Internet, any Web addresses or links contained in this book may have changed since publication and may no longer be valid.

ISBN: 978-1-4401-7355-4 (sc)
ISBN: 978-1-4401-7356-1 (ebk)

Printed in the United States of America

CONTENTS

Dedicated to my parents Philomena and Joe.
Also, dedicated to Star and Chad.

ACKNOWLEDGEMENTS

James Cromie, Chuck Huizenga,
Travis Cohen, Sara Rouch, Joe Ida, Amanda Whitaker,
Dr. Carson Wagner, Professor of Journalism, and
Dr. Robert Whealey, Professor of History.

FOREWORD

The entire landscape of this culture has changed in the past few centuries. Whether it be women's right to vote, the invention of electricity, the landing of men on the moon or innovations in technology, America enters the millennium a very different nation and culture than it was just a century ago. With the socioeconomic and political changes this country has undergone, just about every group's role has changed dramatically to adjust.

One group's role, which has virtually stood still in the changing times, is that of entrepreneurs. It is with sincere hope that this book will change this unfortunate situation. Webster's dictionary explains entrepreneur as a person who organizes and manages an enterprise, especially a business, usually with considerable risk. However, now more than before, surviving the risk of entrepreneurship will be harder than ever due to economic conditions.

The Case for Small Business is divided into two parts; the first of which is then divided into two further sub issues. The sub groupings are comprised of a discussion of problems facing a retailer in today's business landscape, and secondly an exploration into the ways in which these concerns can be alleviated. The last half of the text is dedicated to the development of the National Organization of Retailers with illustrations of sites for national headquarters that is later developed into a self-sustained city.

The book is an attempt to provide a detailed scenario of the pros and cons that befall every owner of small business. The result is a book that gives the beginners a unique and attractive piece of knowledge that they may use in the course of their individual business.

There is no set definition to determine what constitutes a small business. Employing less than fifty employees is generally the accepted criteria for a retailer to be considered a small business. This could be misleading, however. For example, a grocery store that hires fifty people is likely to be a very different kind of establishment than a commercial real estate firm that hires fifty employees.

A better guide would be sales. For example, annual sales of one million dollars or less would constitute a small business. If sales exceed one million dollars but were less than three million, the business could be considered medium-sized. Sales over three million dollars would have to be considered a big business.

The material in this book illustrates many facts that a person could project to become a successful entrepreneur of the future. The author is intending to inform others how to develop a small business and keep the American Dream alive.

Diversity is small business' greatest asset and its biggest weakness. Each business acting individually prevents the establishment from being competitive in the ever-expanding global market.

A National Organization of Retailers would have the ability to become a powerful economic and political force through this new millennium. Under the current structure, our potential goes unrealized.

Lobbyists in Washington, D. C. to represent ideas could persuade legislators to vote for issues favoring small business. There are millions of self employed retailers in America, and any political candidate could use allies.

It is time for retailers to redefine our role in society. Owners of small business must forget the past and gain control of our future. In short, merchants must adjust to survive in a Darwinistic world of the global economy. The new entrepreneurs must develop a business that will produce a greater harmony between family unity and a more prosperous outlook of the twenty-first century. For every owner of small business to retain his/her position, a National Organization for Retailers must be developed.

The main elements for a solid foundation are an excellent administration, base structures and a strong support system. A structure is only as stable as its foundation.

The primary objectives of this text are:

Part I:
1. The decision—Employer or Employee
2. How to successfully operate a business
3. An explanation and understanding of tax forms
4. The need for an association

Part II:
5. Development of the N. O. R.
6. Base structures and support plans
7. Proposals for sites, buildings, and an inter city
8. Constitution—leadership—preamble—purpose—membership—officers—regions—services and by laws

Capitalism is an honorable trait; however, when it extends to greed, capitalism becomes a deadly sin not to be condoned. Greed is the cause destroying American individual businesses. The American Dream wasn't meant to have an individual's loss become another one's personal gain. The true scenario oversees that all people are given a fair chance to succeed without "fat cat" mega-stores debasing smaller shops.

Business owners, united, could redress the dream by enforcing restrictions. Allowing a mega store to come into an area and charge less for merchandise than an independent store can purchase wholesale is ludicrous. A store opening to put others out of business is unethical: thus, taking unfair advantage due to price discrimination.

The Dream has to be redefined so America can put the proper perspective back into practice. Explanations in this book will put emphasis on the essence of family values designating that quality time is 24/7.

Independent retailers not given a fair shake exemplify the cliché that 'life is not fair'. Life itself is fair. People with scrupulous intentions create an atmosphere of unfairness that can be corrected by a National Organization of Retailers (NOR).

INTRODUCTION

The global economy is a complex one. With an ever-growing business world continuing to burgeon, small businesses stand to lose the most. Without the capital or resources necessary to compete with big business, small businesses are forced to stand still in an otherwise expansive age. This has to change. This book explains in detail why small businesses must meet the change, what can (and should) be done to enact the change and what the benefits and consequences will be.

My plans are to illustrate the pros and cons of starting a business, what has to be done for its survival and what is essential to keep the business/family equilibrium.

In writing this book an era of perseverance was the perspective. However, its contribution to owners now and future owners of small business is gratifying.

Part I

The Case for Small Business

This deals primarily with contemporary problems facing small businesses and what they can do to stay competitive in the twenty-first century.

Any successful revolution must begin with a sound plan of action. In business, this strategy is developed through a market study. The results of this study will help us to determine a detailed idea full of development and direction. Soon thereafter, our vision will become a reality.

A short research study involves:

1. Capital—The correct amount of money should not be underestimated. The stakes are far too high to cut corners.
2. Location—Look for a prime location for your establishment.
3. Type of business—For example, retail merchandising or food and beverages being a few of the variety of businesses in which to own and operate. Market size—Number of people already drawn to the area. Who buys? What do they buy? When does customer buy? How can a business encourage more customers to the area, and get buyers to purchase more?
4. Potential Expansion—Expansionism is only possible if there is sufficient room and capital to accommodate it.
5. Managing change—We must envision the future through effective communications, compassion, flexibility, preparation of a common goal with optimizing competent strategies in the use of technology, innovations by trying new ideas skillfully and effectively and following them through until they work.
6. Experience—Positive direction is rewarding. Seek out the experience of other owners of small businesses and add to one's present knowledge. A clear and concise strategy is vital.
7. New Entrepreneur's ability and competency—achieving a successful environment with a constructive image to create customer satisfaction by quickly making prudent decisions and delegating authority. Also key to this, is personnel management—hiring competent and honest employees.
8. Responsibilities—Payroll, budget, management of funds, inventory and sales comparisons or controls, record keeping, bank deposits (day and night), the art of solutions before problems, the ability to solve any new problem that may occur (problem solving) and oversees the complete operation of the business.
9. Taxes—it is a cliché for a person to complain about taxes. In fact, these complaints have become as much an institution as the taxes themselves. Clichés exist for a reason. For every second your business is opened, Uncle Sam is dipping into your cash register. He is not alone. State and local governments are standing in line like vultures trying to seize whatever loose change one might have. With all of these governmental fat cats

pillaging what they can, it is the owners of small business who suffers. That brings us to our first of several diatribes.

Part II

Remedy + Repetition = Reward

It may sound simple, but the only answers that anyone wants to hear to these questions, are solutions. Nobody has the time to continuously hear what all of their problems are. I am quite sure that most of us are well aware of what bothers us. If one is going to resort to repetition, please repeat the positives. They are Remedy + Repetition = Reward! It's the answers, not the questions that need to be repeated. The remedy must be reiterated. If one must resort to redundancy, please have the courtesy of doing so while discussing the solutions.

A National Organization of Retailers would help to ensure that small businesses will no longer be ignored (by the government). An alliance of small businesses laced throughout this land is small business' best hope for ultimate survival.

Part II, Section A presents in detail why N.O.R. is essential to our entire economy. With an organized association, we will all have a voice in Washington. Our businesses will all enjoy unprecedented local, national and international power. Sadly, if the plan for N.O.R. falters so, too, will many of our businesses. It is a classic case of "United We Stand; Divided We Fall."

Section B of Part II will offer a proposal for a National Organization of Retailers. This will include solid base structures, a support system, guidelines, infrastructures, national buildings within a city—all built and constructed by owners of small business.

The purpose of this text is for David to finally be able to compete with Goliath. I aim to help implement a system that rewards classic traits like dedication, hard work, loyalty, ethics and integrity. Entrepreneurs do not need rhetoric and/or false promises. Small businesses need the government to assist them in improving the life of <u>every</u> American.

The bridge in the twenty-first century is narrow and uncertain. If given the opportunity, small businesses may be the only organization with enough diversity, imagination and leadership to lead the way. Together we can leap, not limp into a better tomorrow.

A huge percent of the country's employers own small businesses. Whether your business is local or global, an organization is the fastest way to achieve success. With the correct insight and depth to recognize the immediate need of an association, merchants can reverse the regression and take the movement forward.

Present retailers are the mentors of the new achievers, and must carve a niche that is unparalleled in history. The reader is given substantial information to enhance a better, happier, healthier and meaningful life without retribution. Family attachment with great intensity provides the love and support when ideas are not going your way. Removing ourselves from our families in everyday life by becoming workaholics has many retailers deviating from the norm. Nor was Noel Coward's aphorism meant to separate family and work: "Work is much more fun than fun."

Ethics without distortion is the motivation throughout the text with an emphasis on success and harmony. Business owners working in uniformity solving problems without creating new ones are the dynamics. We can no longer isolate from one another, and expect to survive successfully in the twenty first century. Accomplishing the true significance of life by overcoming all adversity without selling out is the bottom line.

There is monumental hope that you will enjoy the way I utilized the business landscape. Good luck, and may you be among the future's entrepreneurial elite.

CHAPTER 1

Imagine working ten to twelve hours a day without pay. If you are an employer, then you have probably experienced this many times. How did the American Dream become the nightmare that it is? Like any crisis, there are not one but many reasons behind the destruction of the American business.

Most of the current books and magazines that tell one how to start a small business fail to factor in pragmatic solutions for a very real world. A new business that costs less than $50,000 has just a ten percent chance of success. The facts of these "How To" books may be true, but they're not often applicable. These books always seem to forget to warn the new entrepreneur of how difficult it is for one's business to survive.

Although the primary objective is to provide the beginner with some insight on how to survive, it is paramount to understand the obstacles that stand in the way of us all.

Most books are written to earn a profit. This book is no exception. What is different about this book is that the objective is to make this a constructive self-help book for the self-employed individuals and people who are interested in following suit.

The informative "How To" books leave out a very important factor. The overhead (expense of running a business) consumes more time, money and hard work than otherwise imaginable. These facts aren't entirely forthcoming because the expenses aren't complete.

The following information in this book offers many different suggestions involved in successfully managing a small business. Businesses, like people, can be successful regardless of size and resources. In the computer age, businesses can start from one's den without the tremendous overhead expenses that have traditionally plagued them. Expansion is never without consequences. In our zeal to increase our finances, we must remember to continue to spend time with our families. Without strong families throughout this country, our businesses' successes or failures will become secondary. Another consideration for a new business will be leasing the workspace. Even if the business starts off as a home business, if successful, it will eventually require a fresh workspace. Issues such as maintenance, insurance, taxes etc. will all be primary concerns for one's business.

Have you ever read a book or magazine that posed the following questions?

Can you accept responsibility?

Can you make quick and concise decisions?

Do you have an agreeable personality?

Do you get along well with others?

Are you a leader?

"If you do," according to these books and magazine articles, "then you should start a business." While these are all desirable character traits to possess, they do not even begin to scratch the surface of what it takes to be successful in business. The qualities that one must possess are largely intangible. It would be highly improbable, if not impractical to name all of them. Key amongst them, however, is:

Acquisition—the ability to make money
Ambition
Attitude
Changes
Confidence
Competency
Dedication
Discipline
Determination
Ethics
Focus
Good Judgment
Honesty
Integrity

Perseverance
Patience
Personality
Risk
Self-reliance
Self-sufficiency
Time
Vision

Stress Management: Turning bad stress into good feelings—gear the wasted energy into something worthwhile. It works. Aim high and accept who you are. Tolerate Adversity. Deletion is a process of the mind used in the same way as a computer's delete key. Using the delete key the computer can avoid a crash because it has eliminated an overload. It has also left ample room for ramification of new ideas. Practice deletion. The mind will substitute delete for stress. The individual no longer believes in stress channeling the open space of the mind for constructive energy and meaningful thought.

Depression is no more than an accumulation of past failures. Feeling sorry for one's self doesn't help either. The more failures one may have, the deeper the depression. This too can be eliminated by deletion. Delete failures from the mind. Do not overreact. As depletion works for the removal of stress it can also be used to replace negative thought.

You cannot repress—you must renounce. You can call the process mind renovation—delete by cleaning out the debris or the garbage that the mind may have stored. Now, restore the mind to its original emptiness. The mind is now opened for new knowledge and experience.

The main obstacle is fulfilling the empty part of the mind with the new positive believing technique. Do not rush. It will come in time. Use the deletion process as much as necessary.

Now, with practice as you pass through life you'll know how to delete, restore and move on. Therefore delete any new stress or depression as it may occur. I call this psychological replacement. Hurrying the process will run you into difficulty. Delete it over and over until the restoration is complete. Continuous practice as time goes on will have you functioning as quickly as the delete key removes excess on a computer.

Delete, delete, delete—restore to emptiness—add new knowledge and experience.

The above list of terms is worth remembering when owning and operating a small business in the global economy.

The most difficult task for any business can be its primary goal, which is simply staying out of debt and accumulating a profit. Balancing the budget and working without a deficit are essential. Any small business that attempts to operate on a deficit is also operating on borrowed time. Small businesses will not be bailed out by any government agency. Even if the government did try to intervene, owners of small business should be very reluctant to accept their help. Like banks, government loans operate on interest. **A debt is a debt is a debt.**

People go into small business for a consortium of reasons; thus, mine was that I enjoyed working with the public. Owning a local business gave me the opportunity to make a living and meet new people at the same time. Little did I know that opening my own business did not free me as hoped? Instead, it shackled me with an entire set of new responsibilities and constraints levied by higher powers.

These government regulations are nobly intended. Like everything else the government does, the result is a one sided compromise to a suit antiquated notions and regulations. Perhaps the most offensive compromise is the principles and morals of the entrepreneurs.

Though false as it may seem, you are merely a puppet dancing on a string. "Uncle Sam" and his cronies are masterful puppeteers. An author of the Elizabethan era once suggested, "We are merely the stars' tennis balls tossed and blown whichever way pleases them most." I've altered it to create more meaningful and illustrative impact. This statement will ring true throughout one's life and throughout this book.

Everyday, small-business owners act as the proverbial battered wives of the federal government. We are used, abused and cast aside in direct accordance with their whims.

The federal government levies strict financial penalties against any business that makes even a marginal error in their records. These findings may cripple a small business. It is not unreasonable to ask the government to grant a shopkeeper a minimal period of time, so the owner of small business is able to rectify his/her error. Owning one's business often ends up as a thankless job for efforts contributing to the welfare of others.

If knowledge is power, this book will equip you for the rigors of dealing with the government. This autonomous control must be challenged and changed.

When the whole concept of organizing began in this country, the slogan was: "United we stand; divided we all fall." Self-employed are in such a position right now. Local merchants, now in dire emotional straits, have become sanctioned sweatshop workers; thus, a modern day version of indentured slavery. If we fail to join with each other, our incomes, status, power and societal roles will continue to decrease. Conversely, if we can join forces, our collective voice will be heard throughout the world. A word of kindness on a job well done would be sufficient. The government is incapable of such compassion or warmth. We need to change that. A kinder, gentler nation would be more appealing.

A 1991 ultimatum had President Bush give Congress 100 days to present a bill on highways and crime. They easily failed to meet this deadline on some very important issues. There were no repercussions. If you or I fail to meet set deadlines, we are assessed a financial penalty. The government appears to be playing by different rules. The President relented on the issue granting Congress more time to further examine all the issues. Congress should take a similar road in dealing with small business. Our growth as an entity needs the support, not opposition of higher forces. Small-business owners and their employees provide a majority of all taxes collected by the government. Our success or failure is of extreme importance to this country.

The government is a misleading term. We tend to think of government as all the people, but it is only made up of a few lawmakers that represent the total population. There are really several loosely tied ruling bodies that effectively determine the speed and tenor of our culture. Public office seems to attract a certain type of personality. Every small-business owner wonders at some point, "Am I paying taxes to serve the country, or am I paying taxes to be harassed, used and abused?" All too often the conclusion has been the latter.

When running one's own business, the shop owner has to take orders from just about everywhere. The owner is responsible for all of the businesses' operations. This gives him/her control, but does it give him/her power? I think not.

In stark contrast, a person who is employed can master skills and perform his/her job without interruption. It would seem that they also have control.

There is an existing organization set up by the federal government—American Small Business Association. Like most government organizations, it almost always proves unsatisfactory. In fact, I haven't known anyone to gain any type of satisfaction from the SBA; however, that doesn't mean someone hasn't. I wonder if this agency is just another waste of taxpayer money.

We have already gone through some very important facts on small business. We are not free, and we do have a boss. We have also discussed the ineffectiveness of government bureaucracy. Owners of small businesses are forced to tap dance and juggle at the same time. It is now time that we discuss our strengths. The advantage lies in our pure numbers.

The small-business owner must manage money and people. In addition to dealing with constant bureaucratic interference, a current entrepreneur must be able to cope with the demands and whims of an increasingly expectant work force as well. Obviously, the most important key to the successful launching of a new business is a strong financial base from which to draw. If you lack the money initially, you will soon be in the red.

The odds of failure today are much greater due to a number of factors. They include: inflation, recessions, varying interest rates, increasingly higher payroll, inflated payroll taxes, a wavering world economy and the overall bureaucracy. It would seem that with each passing year the government adds a new form or two to the existing epic that is the tax report. War and Peace seems to have far fewer pages than my tax report (It's also much more interesting). Cutting through this proverbial red tape, by spending countless hours accounting for trivial moments in one's financial past is both intrusive and counter-productive. In essence, it is a government mandate that the business owner spend most of his/her time recording past affairs rather than exploring new and creative ones. Our nation has a deficit that we can never pay off.

Bureaucracy harbors complacency. Every example of the government poking its nose into private affairs bares the same characteristics. They are almost always genuinely well intended and invariably never work. People who are calling for a National Health Care program are not looking at the whole picture.

If this huge entity has screwed up everything it has ever regulated, what leads one to believe that this time will be any different? Perhaps the most outrageous of the existing litany of failed governmental intervention lies with the minimum wage.

When one works at a set rate of speed, that rate is almost certain to diminish if one is not motivated by sales incentives. The minimum wage has bred an atmosphere of complacency. It is rare for any employee to work to his/her full potential because this system has taught them otherwise. If an employer is required to pay an employee a minimum wage, the employer should be afforded the same luxury. This is not to say that an employee wins in this situation either.

If the minimum wage were to be raised one dollar per hour, the taxes would equate to nearly 25%. In addition to the six to eight percent sales tax that is standard in most states, the government is pilfering nearly 33% of one's alleged bonus. Suddenly, the dollar raise that one thought he or she was receiving is actually closer to a sixty-seven cent raise.

The business must compensate for this new financial strain. The natural solution is for the business to subsequently raise the price of items to help cover its loss. If you keep prices down to encourage volume, it can become a lost cause. Consequently, the employee/consumer is trading a sixty-seven cents increase for a dollar deficit. Therefore, the minimum wage serves to further subjugate its recipients.

A set wage has hurt everyone. They have hurt the employer, the employee and the overall economy. Instead of seven people working at one dollar an hour, the minimum wage has forced the employer to hire one person at seven dollars an hour. The result is a shrinking and less productive work force.

Retailers simply cannot compete with the wages and benefits offered by large corporations. Seven dollars an hour is easily affordable to companies like McDonald's or Sears. Conversely, it can be quite steep to a neighborhood shop trying to make ends meet.

Loaning money to small businesses is a racket much like the college loan. It only serves to drive up interest rates so that yet more revenue can be extracted for the lender. Some moneys must be allocated to encourage growth, not discourage it. While money is divided among worthy causes, small business is not one of them. If small business is the backbone of the American economy, then why aren't merchants among the government's revenue sharing arrangement?

The government shut down in December of 1995. Amazingly, this actually did not hurt the pocketbooks of the federal employees. Instead, they were being paid while not on the job, and at the same time the oval office was used to entertain. The tax money extorted from small businesses went afoul.

While the government "fat cats" were away, it was the individual shop owners who were forced to pay. The tax money extorted from small businesses was largely responsible for the funds that paid these federal employees. Along with tolls levied by creditors and other expenses, there is nothing left for the employer.

There has to be a solution to this serious problem. An organization for entrepreneurs may serve to rectify this crisis. Business people should not have to pay the price so everyone else can play on the merry-go-round. This is especially true when the employer has people under him/her that are deserving of pay.

Financial compensation for an employer is needed who works an average of twelve hours a day for nothing. There is no method to the government's madness.

One of the worst words in the English language is "bankruptcy." To a business owner, the very word conjures up their worst fears. Without the proper support, many hard and honest workers will continue to battle with this merciless beast.

Absolutely no disrespect or disparagement is intended for any other profession. In fact, many are admired and respected for what they have accomplished. The purpose of the book is to help to model a small business organization after existing associations. Retailers should be granted the same freedoms and amenities as everyone else.

There was a time in this country's not so distant past that one could walk into a bank, request a loan, sign a contract or two and go home with money in hand. This is no longer a reality. Today's borrower must fill out a litany of agreements, and endure very close personal scrutiny. One has to decide which will make him/her emotionally more stable, the money or the privacy.

There are costly disasters with no relief. The 1990's savings and loan bailout by the federal government only further illustrates the magnanimous difference between how the government deals with big business versus how it controls small businesses. It is unlikely the government would lift a finger to ever help a small business, while it has proven that it will jump through hoops to salvage larger ones. Still, it is paramount that one not be intimidated. Go for it! It is still possible for one to be a successful entrepreneur. It is just more trying now than ever before. Other professions are advancing faster, paying better and more stable because they have all well organized themselves. The National Organization of Retailers would be a giant step towards closing the existing gap.

The words consistency and fairness are not relevant to store owners. Owning a shop of any kind entails countless unpaid hours, no benefits, an unstable and uncertain Social Security, seemingly endless bookwork, expenses and the necessity of relying on the fancies of others for one's own survival. This is indigenous of all product related fields. All of these factors boil down to one word—**RISK**.

Risk is a natural part of any job these days. With the economy as volatile and inconsistent as it has been, no job is safe. Many people think that the best way to avoid risk and control their destiny, is to run their own business. What is bitterly ironic about this is, these people often evacuate a bad situation in favor of a worse one. They find that the dream of personal freedom, prosperity and security has been usurped with the reality of government-imposed financial shackles, economic uncertainty and a sea of debt.

The obvious question that any reader must have is, "If things are so dire, why stay with it? If everything is bad, why don't I get out?" The answer is simple. I believe in small independent business as the driving force in our economy. People with my experience must continue to fight the good fight so that our nation's youth can one day to succeed in enterprise.

All revolutions are fraught with casualties. This one will be no different. Some businesses, by their own refusal, may not survive this transformation to organization. How is that any different than the myriad of businesses that are exterminated everyday because of their refusal or inability to comply with the arbitrary and often contradictory shims of properly implemented laws? The result very well may be financial and professional success beyond anything currently conceivable.

You have a chance of being successful. This book was written for you. It offers constructive, pragmatic and suggestive material for those who chose to use it. There are many issues and problems that require addressing from new and established businesses alike.

If at times, this book seems repetitious, it is. Repetition is the best way to describe any retailer's tedious work day. Whether with one's customers or one's employees, constantly repeating one's self is a regular part of any successful employer's job.

With repetition being such an intricate part of the day, it is only natural that a book geared at that group be similarly formatted. Some points must be reiterated to prove that they are relevant in many aspects of this profession. If you can bare with the redundancy, you will enjoy and benefit from this reading. Words like harassment, taxes, abusers of power and bureaucratic controls are all central themes to this book.

The following is a list of some useful terms to memorize and apply when or if one chooses to become an entrepreneur. One can develop one's own connotations to these words as they appear throughout the text:

Benefits
Building design
Capital
Caring
Compassion
Confidence
Constructive communication
Courage
Customer availability
Customer satisfaction
Decisions
Discounts/sales
Enjoyment
Experience

Global economy
Happiness
Humor
Innovation
Kindness
Knowledge
Location
Management
Opening/closing hours
Operating expenses
Outside considerations
Payroll
Potential expansion
Profit
Promotions
Respect
Retailing
Sacrifice
Sales-volume
Supply/demand
Taxes
Time/work/energy
Understanding
Vision
Weather
Working conditions

Intimate understanding of the aforementioned words will help give one a basic grasp of what is necessary to begin and maintain a successful and lucrative business. An honest day's work does not always mean an honest day's pay. As there is in everyday life unexpected setbacks do happen.

On a very good day the employer's paycheck may be highly rewarding. Some days may not be financially rewarding, however, one may develop lasting friendships and good conversation. Interpersonal relationships become an asset when owning your own business. The customer will have to start and finish the conversation.

Chapter 2

Technology

Technology has facilitated the exponential growth of our society. Inventions like the microwave oven and the computer have had profound effects on how our society functions. Living in the "Information Age" has had its drawbacks as well, however. The rapid pace that capitalism has forced is helping to eliminate some of the cornerstones of our culture.

Books are a good example of this. When Johann Gutenberg invented the printing press in 1463, the history of the written word would forever be altered. Nowhere is that better underscored than in our present computer oriented culture. By the time many books came out, they were already outdated. Concepts and ideas that are viable in one month may be obsolete in the next. Gutenberg's revolutionary invention allowed for curiosity amongst the people to grow. With the common person able to obtain books, mostly bibles, knowledge and change were but a foregone conclusion.

The Internet offers a modern-day equivalent to Gutenberg's printing press. Just as learning how to effectively utilize the printing press was Europe's bride from the Dark Ages into the Renaissance, computer proficiency is a vital instrument for our social and professional advancement.

The church autocratically and arbitrarily ruled the fifteenth century. The empowerment of the common man through literacy helped to change all that. Again, we have reached an historical crossroad. If we choose to use this immensely powerful resource, we will all become more powerful than ever before. If we choose not to take advantage of this considerable opportunity, we will have done ourselves a disservice.

Computer awareness in conjunction with the continued use of books will give the aspiring entrepreneur advanced insights into the basics and nuances of beginning a business. Consequently, the Internet can be used from any location provided your business initiates a mailing service. The computer used by business owners adds a whole new dimension to the word location.

Some general facts to consider are listed:

1. Plenty of working <u>capital</u> is necessary to fund any business. Capital serves as the metaphoric foundation of the business financial structure. Without a strong and sound economic base, the business cannot succeed. This common base will be required for: advertising, insurance, inventory/stock, loans, materials/supplies, rent, repairs, taxes, utilities, equipment and wages.
2. Giving broad tips to prospective entrepreneurs can often be ineffective. What is successful for one business may not necessarily be as fruitful for another. A good example of this is with <u>competition</u>. The prevailing school of thought once held that the less competition one had, the more prosperous his/her business would be. Later market surveys found that many people who ordinarily would not have shopped at certain stores were more likely to do so if one had a convenient alternative. The results of these findings led to things like fast food establishments sprouting up near each other and of course the insurgence of shopping malls. Competition can be good or bad depending on the circumstances. Small-business owners must change with the times to remain successful; therefore, it is advisable to know the competition's long-term effect. This involves **risk** taking.
3. It has been said that the three most important elements for a business to succeed are, <u>location</u>, <u>location</u>, <u>location</u>. The percentage of traffic one can generate in his/her store is a direct determinant of how much revenue the store can garner. A

retailer may have the best ideas and products in the world, but if one's location is poor, likely so too is their business.

4. Another simple factor in our economy is the relationship between <u>supply and demand</u>. If a market exists for any product that is economically viable, any merchant is remiss if he/she fails to meet that need. Few businesses choose to ignore the whims of the public. It is just exceedingly difficult to figure out exactly what they do and do not want. Sales are a fickle business.

    In business, as in life, one's ability to adapt to <u>change</u> is a crucial element to his/her success. Controlled changes have to be considered repeatedly. This means changes that may be necessary on a temporary or permanent basis to protect the welfare of the establishment. These changes are often necessary to increase sales, fight off competition and to keep customers interested.

5. Owners of small businesses must spend <u>time</u> wisely. Unfortunately, financial circumstances often dictate that one spend more time at his/her business than with his/her respective families. It has become a catch 22 situation. If you want to provide for your family, you must neglect them. If you choose not to neglect your family, you must take time off from your business. That may be just as bad because you run the risk of hurting your family financially. This problem is not indigenous to business employers. The current economic climate has generated this conflict nearly across the board. A solution must be reached.

    It has been said that Dolly Parton's *Nine to Five* is the anthem of the working person. I would guess that any small-business owner would walk the globe for such hours. Our song would be more like the Beatles' *A Hard Day's Night* or even *Eight Days a Week*. This rigorous schedule has prompted many business owners to decide to 'Take This Job and Shove It.'

6. How many <u>hours</u> per day will the business be open? This is an excellent question that may not be easy to determine. Many businesses are now opting to stay opened for 24 hours

a day. **24/7** cannot be under estimated. If that option is not financially possible, a shopkeeper must choose wisely his/her operating hours. Regardless of his/her choice, one can bet that they will put in a great many more hours than ever imagined.

For every second that one's business is not opened, the business is losing money. Expenses such as rent, utilities, loan interest and other costs add up quickly. Business owners understand this fact all too well. By not being open they know that they cannot make money on what they cannot sell. Therefore the longer they are open, the better the chances of improving sales. This mentality may lead to a short-term gain but often results in the owner's personal demise. No human being can or should live that way. The chapter entitled, "Getting Started Financially" will elaborate further on this point and address ways to rectify this.

7. Bringing us to a bit of a brainteaser. In life and business, one must accept the negatives with the positives. This means that although negative, the thought is positive by recognizing the negative. Thus, the self-employed must develop a technique to counter balance the unproductive hours. Do you understand that? Good.

Philosophically speaking—Time has always been an arbitrary demarcation by which we judge the changes of society, and though at times it may seem subjective, it is the only analog we have. When we apply this model to what we might refer to as an era, we see a slow trend of almost indiscernible events, seamless in their passing, that eventually spell out the map of progress and transformation, but only when they are taken apart from their linage and studied as independent of any chronology that has not been severely fragmented.

In the last fifty years our nation has spawned a momentum of change, dynamic in its proportions, unrivaled by even that of the sheer expanse of the past two hundred years and comparable to that of the period of rebirth in a Europe emerging from the clutches of the Dark Ages.

Whether it is the invention of electricity, the issue of woman's suffrage, the landing of man on the moon or a wireless Internet, America entered the millennium a very different nation and culture than it was just a century ago. Nearly every sect of American society has shifted dramatically. It is with sincere hope that this book will help to change the unfortunate dilemma of retailers across the United States that has resulted from the inability to cope with this change.

8. <u>Change</u> is not forthcoming unless time is taken into focus on a united way of life. In order for a better tomorrow we cannot operate as we have in the past. "United we stand, divided we fall." Change represents an element that is vital for small business survival. Technology has provided us with new directions in which to present and implement our innovations. We must use this strategy when facing challenges in the future by our ample numbers.

9. Many critical <u>elements</u> outside the business must be considered before one invests all of his/her time and money. Chief among them may be, well the elements. Weather is always a factor connected to business sales. The more inclement the weather, the slower the business will be. If the weather is favorable, however, so too will be your sales. Snow and ice can be treacherous. Their reputation for making life difficult is often enough to keep people from traveling. This is not good news for the owner of a shop. A 10 to 15 hours day can seem twice as long to the shopkeeper who has watched his/her business operate at a loss due to foul weather.

10. <u>Honesty</u> is a major trait. America is starving for leaders of substantial traits. In a society that breeds leaders with traits such as, lies, denial, cover-up, wrongdoing, corruption, misuse of funds, leaders who lack integrity and ethics, Americans need the priorities once spoken and implemented by the likes of Abraham Lincoln. Leaders of quality are leaders of compassion, truth and ethics.

It is not going to be easy locating the ideal employee for an owner of any establishment. Employers hiring people who are hard working, industrious, dependable, compatible and honest is tough. It boils down to integrity.

Employee theft is a far greater threat to an employer than customer pilfering. It threatens to destroy the entire atmosphere of trust that is essential in running a small business. It leads all shopkeepers to seek ways to prevent its existence. Thomas Edison once said, "Prevention is ninety percent of the cure." The same holds true for business. The best theft deterrent is hiring the right people. Any foundation that is not build on integrity, ethics and honesty will lose luster, and has nil chance of survival.

Some measures must be taken to help regulate one's business. Perhaps the most effective device may be the oldest one. A daily record of sales and inventory helps to not only count the existing merchandise, but it also serves as a strict deterrent to any potential internal-thieves. Another way to prevent theft is to provide incentives to any employee who catches another worker stealing. One's colleagues are often the best detectives.

A large supermarket chain failed to notice a large embezzling campaign with one of the chain's more prominent employees. Other employees within the company had noticed that the pirate had been sporting luxuries and amenities that did not seem to fit into his economic strata. They soon notified the organization's powers at large. A subsequent trap was set, in which the embezzler took the bait, hook, line and sinker.

This person was caught and dismissed from his duties. The business was fortunate to have loyal and dedicated employees. Not all businesses are as fortunate. Many times, the unmitigated theft that has become so common in our culture, can lead to the financial ruin of a fragile small business. One out of every business is doomed for failure due to employee thief. Retailers cannot let other's dishonesty determine their destiny.

A task force of investigators may be set up to help assist employers. Their job would be to go from business to business trying to determine where (if any) theft is being committed in a store. This is just one of many advantages a unified retailers association would provide. Security is of extreme importance. A National Organization of Retailers collectively could pull together enough resources to hire the best theft detectives in the business. With the advent of the security camera law enforcers have an added tool to help them fight crime. Video cameras have done a good job in helping to curb this problem, but the next step has yet to be taken.

Theft is and has been a problem for shop owners for as long as small businesses themselves. A 1997 USA Today poll found that as many as 48% of all Americans had stolen from and/or lied to their employers within the past year. The article went on to suggest, "If you haven't lied to or stolen from your boss, chances are the person next to you has."

Through modern technology there has to be a much better way to eliminate theft. However, as people we must keep our morals, ethics and values intact. As business people we must not despair. The advancement of technology to further assist retailers will arrive in due process.

The sudden spread of many administrators and leaders of higher education, who are unfortunately relying on telling untruths to achieve their goal, have past the unimportance of ethics, honesty and integrity to the minds of students seeking a formal education; thus, preparing us with new leaders of false substance and misguidance. A shaken and un-solid foundation for individuals paying close to $100,000 for a four year education is ludicrous beyond anyone's imagination. Young scholars deserve better.

Solutions, later in this book, will provide a way for retailers to recoup losses financially. At present, if the taxes, bookwork and government intervention does not destroy retailers; the honesty factor will send him/her to depths unknown.

Do not despair, though. Relief will be offered in the second part of this book. Remedy, remedy, remedy to all small business problems will be the analytical component in an everlasting economy.

Remedy + Repetition = Reward

Chapter 3

Employer or Employee

Employer or Employee: That is the question that we all must answer for ourselves. Whether one is an aspiring entrepreneur, an experienced business owner or neither, at some point just about everyone considers self-employment. Each dreams of the proverbial *pot o' gold* that may await them at the end of their economic rainbow. Hopefully, we have dispelled any myth of something for nothing in American business—there is no such pot. We all know this in our heads; unfortunately, our hearts refuse to yield to such sound logic. Each year, thousands cast aside their previous lives to pursue their respective American Dreams. Some succeed—most do not. Examining why this happens and what can be done to improve the percentage of success is key to the development of small business. It is also the prevailing theme of this chapter.

Who has better working conditions, a more substantial salary and better benefits: an employer or employee? The answer may not be as obvious as one might think. Independent business people establish their salary by the success of their business. Working conditions are whatever can be afforded. If one's place of business is a dump, his/her business will feel the sting. The nicer a place looks, the more likely it is to be patronized. This leads to the topic of benefits. Perks like health insurance, dental care, sick leave, and paid vacation are but a dream for the small-business owner.

If you are treading water to stay afloat, you can't afford to rest your legs. Regardless of how tired your legs become, you must keep kicking. The situation has eroded into a lose/lose proposition for owners. If retailers do not run themselves into the ground physically, the business climate will surely do it financially.

In a capitalistic society, there will always be some jobs that pay more for less work and better benefits than others. That is just a consequence of a free market. It is also one of the hallmarks of our culture. Free-market capitalism is not the problem; governmental intervention is. Big Brother continues to meddle in all of the affairs of small business. Everything is regulated and monitored. Without any of the amenities of free trade, bureaucratic control by our government can serve no purpose other than to stifle otherwise successful business. The reason for this is simple. Small business makes for an easy, disorganized and passive target. Without a political voice of our own, we will continue to be destined for unnecessary regulations. In stark contrast, some vocations and professions have become so powerful that they help to dictate what the government does rather than the other way around. In admiration of their achievements, it's proof that owners of small businesses with the lobbyists in Washington, D.C. could get where individual shop owners want to go. For the sake of illustration, let's discuss a few.

PART I

Education vs. Business

The principle purpose of education is to pass on the values and social norms of our ancestors to future generations through *traditions, experience* and *knowledge*. This understanding of who we are will allow us to better understand the world in which we live.

The average elementary and secondary school teacher's pay factored in with the average administrator's pay, results in an annual salary of about 35,000 dollars. Along with another estimate of roughly 10,000 additional dollars in benefits, it can be safe to say that teachers have well organized themselves. The result has been nothing less than breathtaking.

Most schools are required to operate a minimum of 180 days a year. That means that a teacher who works everyday of the year still only works a total of about half of the year. If one factors in sick days, personal days and days off resulting from inclement weather, it is entirely feasible that a teacher may work for less than half the year. If the teacher is able to establish tenure, sabbatical absences may also follow suit. Tenure also allows for better job security. Perhaps no other profession in this country boasts comparable benefits, working hours and job stability.

The one major advantage that small-business owners do enjoy is that the more experience and education a small-business owner has the more money he/she is likely to make. This is not necessarily true with teachers. With more education, they become less attractive financially to prospective employers. Though governmental regulations have standardized wages for teachers with varying levels of education this sometimes works against the teachers. School districts will often hire the less expensive applicant regardless of the qualification. This trend has led to many teachers being forced to stay in jobs for much longer than they desire. This may help to explain the state of education in our country. If the teacher is bored with the subject matter, why shouldn't the kids be? A stagnant teacher is likely to be an ineffective one.

This is by no means a disparagement of the teaching profession. Organizations such as the National Education Association have done yeoman's work in advancing the profession financially. With each passing year they are properly becoming better and better compensated. With a new tax bracket comes new responsibilities, however. With the systematic destruction of the nuclear family; teachers serve as surrogate parents to their students now more than ever. If one can deal with the profession's pressures, then teaching would make an excellent career.

PART II

Education vs. Business

To become a professor at a university, one must generally obtain his/her Ph.D. But at least a graduate degree, although terminal degrees are most preferred. If one is fortunate enough to attain a position working for a college or university as an administrator, one could earn a salary of anywhere between five and six figures. That is before one even factor's in any other benefits (i.e. medical, dental, retirement etc.). Some of these benefits may surprise you. The typical work-a-day university president has a free home, a guest house, a help staff, catered food, free access to air transportation, (most have their own airplane at the expense of the university), expert health care, excellent retirement and free office expenses all at the state's expense. Not a bad way to live.

The average college or university professor earns around $108,749 (United States Department of Labor, 2009. Due to a lag in time salaries that are mentioned throughout the book may vary). Professors too, have free office space and excellent incentives. Among a professor's myriad of benefits are the facts that his/her children are invited to attend the same college or university free of charge. With the cost of college sky-rocketing as it is, this becomes a more and more valuable benefit.

College professors differ from primary and secondary educators in a litany of ways. Chief amongst them are their day's structure. A high school teacher may spend between six and eight hours in the same room, doing nothing but teaching. A college professor may teach up to three consecutive hours on any given day, but very rarely any more. It is unusual for any college professor to spend more than two to three hours daily in the classroom. The rest of their day may be spent on planning lessons, grading papers, partying with students or faculty, writings or writing books. If a university or college requires a professor to spend more time on a research paper than a class lesson plan; what does that imply about student's value of education? Less value is placed on teaching as opposed to research.

One area where college professors must be commended on, however, is their ability to garner good wages and benefits without having to unionize. They remain one of the few professions that can boast such a feat. Of course, this is only possible at the taxpayers' expense. Without the amount of local, state, and federal funding that these institutions receive, most colleges and universities would be far less liberal with their salary and work structures.

A common theme amongst college and university administrators is to bellyache about the increasingly low standards at which high school students are being taught. The colleges and universities complain that their increasing dropout rates are due in large part to their students being under prepared when they arrive. The problem with this logic is that it was those same colleges and universities that produced the teachers who are educating the students.

There can be no doubt that our nation's education system is not as effective as it once was. There are a gaggle of theories as to why this is so. Some contend that most of our learning occurs in the home. With the traditional family going the way of the eight-track tape player, the children suffer the most. While kids from past generations could focus their concentration on baseball cards and cartoons, current kids are more likely to deal with sexual sessions on the Internet and feeding themselves after school. Others claim the kids are amazingly resilient. They are able to overcome just about anything. Unfortunately, poor formal education isn't one of them. Both are probably half right in their assertions.

The following points being made do not apply to professors that are devoted to their profession. Substantiating the theory—student's inability to meet college standards, a short research was conducted concerning the college education of high school teachers. It was found out that colleges had not competently prepared the present teachers; thus, what is occurring:

1. University administration focuses more on industrial workshops instead of a higher learning institution. No ethics here.
2. Student's classroom time was limited. Classes are cancelled or dismissed before the required scheduled class time.
3. Individual students have little if any personal time with professors.
4. A personal conflict between a student and his/her professor had developed.
5. Some students have been doing their observation in a different field of study: (ex. future secondary educators doing observation in preschool)
6. Professors busy writing books; thus, they often find teaching annoying.
7. A student claimed a 3.2 grade point average without attending one class the whole term. He explained how it was accomplished.
8. Much time given to sport programs allowing sports to take precedence over academics.

9. Before the recession, college administrators were getting yearly double-digit salary increases, and professors getting high single-digit increases sometimes regardless of performances. Administrators were getting raises while the universities were losing money. This is unfair to the educators teaching by the old rules and taking an interest in their student's progress.

10. Trustees and administrators more interested in financial worth of college than a student's progress.

11. Presidents spend fifty percent of the time raising funds and the other half as academic leadership on campus. Presidents used to spend one hundred percent of time in academic leadership. One wonders where these presidents were educated. Again greed has replaced Capitalism.

12. Washington (AP)—First lady, Laura Bush, wanted college educators to better prepare new teachers. Mrs. Bush says a college education does not necessarily prepare students to become teachers, and that teachers who find themselves unprepared should let their former professors know.

Bush wants to encourage teachers to write back to their educators and say, "These things were really valuable and these weren't, and I wish I'd been prepared to do this or that." These are noble intentions.

However, this just simply doesn't work. The type of teacher/professor communications she advocates has been done to no avail. Were not these professors once young themselves? Another example of how ineffective political influence can be.

After spending over one hundred thousand dollars and four years of learning, a teacher needs the entire energy one has and any work that takes them away from their students is a detriment. This is a problem to be solved by professors not necessarily teachers. If educators of higher learning want to send out questionnaires and explore the field that's fine. You want to go one step further. Aside from dedicated professors, the problem is the professor and the professors who taught them.

Elementary and secondary school teachers are not responsible for the inadequate education they received from their college professors (as if teachers need more required work). Asking the student what he/she has learned or not learned in a class is hardly a solution to anything.

That is why tests are given. As a qualified teacher the first lady knows that a teacher's responsibility is difficult as it is. The problem is more serious needing many remedies on the part of professors not dedicated to the profession.

In researching the college atmosphere, we found that the predicament has been around for many years without being solved. The research took very little time and accomplished considerable information. If the eleven points the author has given were corrected, it would remedy this problem of irresponsibility.

To relate in retrospect when I was in college, my high school coach was on campus for the day, and stopped and asked me if I was having a problem in English. Told him grades were just above average.

Coach said that the university had notified the school because university students from my high school were having problems in English. I responded, "Sounds like the professors were incompetent preparing teachers to teach high school English." He laughed and said, "You're right." The smile on his face assured me that he was relieved of any guilt that may have been apparent. Solution accomplished.

College years at one time had sixteen weeks of study with a week of finals. Today, semesters are around fourteen weeks and a week of finals. Therefore paying a year's rent in private housing is unjustified when only living in the apartment thirty weeks out of the year. It is unfair to the lessee.

PART III

Non-Academic College Employees vs. Business

It is not unusual for a college student to try and secure a job at his/her alma mater. Why not? Hourly wages regularly hover around twelve dollars per hour with a package of benefits that would make most people break into cartwheels. Though non-academic professionals, employees are usually offered free tuition and free tuition for all members of the family while employed by the college or university.

Medical Practice vs. Business

The American Medical Association is one of the strongest, most unified organizations in the United States. A.M.A. members hail from a variety of different fields and backgrounds within the medical community. Their faith in the association holds it together. Currently, they enjoy all of the amenities and luxuries of a huge association. They owe this to a number of factors. One of these factors is that the A.M.A. has an excellent staff of lobbyists. According to Webster's Dictionary, "a lobbyist is one employed by an organization to influence legislators to introduce or vote for measures favorable to the interests' one represents." These power brokers often help to decide who runs the country and how he/she governs. A good example of this is with a national health care system.

Though public opinion polls seemed to overwhelmingly support the plan, it never had a legitimate chance. Strong organizations with skilled and influential lobbyists were able to thwart the bid before it ever reached a serious vote. Where do you suppose the A.M.A. stood on a free national health care plan?

Despite a strong association, most doctors still put in long arduous hours only to suffer from the same scrutiny and agitation of governmental intervention.

This constant badgering seems to limit their time in research, so that they can follow all of the trivial bureaucratic forms to the letter.

Physicians, like owners of small businesses, are also billed for just about every feasible expense. Building, office, staff and equipment are just some of the expenditures of doctors who are not affiliated with hospitals. Doctors who operate out of hospitals are fortunate in that they are able to concentrate on their jobs, instead of worrying about book keeping. Hospitals also are better equipped to shield their doctors from the increasing number of malpractice suits being filed. With the protection of their stability, however, hospitals also serve to intervene into every aspect of their employees' practice(s). In this way, they are exactly like our government. Hospital doctors have more commitments than physicians in private practice and usually do not earn the same degree of pay as those in private practice.

The medical field is a unique one. One can choose to be an employer or employee depending on which is more lucrative. Many are choosing the latter over the former because of the superior benefits, little bookwork and legal refuge of hospitals. Some doctors practice with other doctors in what is called a clinic, therefore sharing the expenses.

However, for every minute a doctor spends filling out forms is time taken away from patient treatment.

Nursing vs. Business

To become a *Registered Nurse* (RN), one must pass a minimum of two years of schooling to attain one's associate degree. This is not a bad deal considering that the average nurse begins at about $28,000-$33,000 per year. A staff nurse may also enjoy the benefits like a partial or full reimbursement for continuance of their education. Full hospitalization and full retirement are also perks that a registered nurse may enjoy. Perhaps the biggest advantage of nursing is the extended paid vacation time. Some RN's may earn up to four weeks of paid vacation. The benefits that nurses enjoy are well documented. What is not as renowned and known are the benefits that nurses' families enjoy. They also get free health care for being related to a registered nurse. Due to the fact that there is no national health care program (or one that is acceptable by everyone) free health care is an important family benefit.

Law vs. Business

For an attorney to practice law legally, he/she must hold an undergraduate degree from an accredited university as well as attending a three-year ABA accredited law school. From there the aspiring lawyer must take and pass the litigation's bar examination. It simply tests the young lawyer's knowledge of his/her respective state law, as well as a smaller portion known as the multi-state, testing over more broad constitutional and federal issues of the law.

This test is very complex and requires a great deal of studying. It also varies from state to state. West Virginia and Virginia's bar may be very different. A few states have what is known as a reciprocity agreement with one or more states, in which the passing of the state's bar enables that person to practice law in any state with which that state has the reciprocity agreement. However, this is not the norm, and it is for this reason that most lawyers only practice in one state.

Many never do pass the bar examination. It can be that difficult. One of the strange things about law school is that the information for which the bar examination is taught in the first year of a three year program; thus one of the main causes for the difficulty encountered with the bar exam. For those who are fortunate enough to pass the test, however, the advantages can be untold. One such advantage is immediate membership into one of Washington D.C.'s strongest lobbies, The American Bar Association.

No lobby is strong enough to eliminate bureaucracy. Like all business owners, self-employed attorneys are loaded down with a litany of paperwork to meet the governmental standards. Add this to a profession that already requires a great deal of time spent writing and researching and it has become a mess.

According to a 1991 Los Angeles Times survey conducted by Maura Dolan, "lawyers have been more affected by alcoholism, drug abuse and depression than any other profession."

Dolan states another factor that has negatively impacted law—the pressure to win. Trials have degenerated from an open discourse used to determine the relative innocence or guilt of an accused person to a verbal equivalent of a three-ring circus. The result has been an overall loss of respect for lawyers by the general public.

There is an obvious question out of all of this. Why do so many lawyers seem so distraught with their profession? Dolan's survey concludes "that many attorneys claim that their unhappiness is linked to the job itself." The constant pressure to win has usurped the noble principles of pursuing justice. For many, the result has been a great increase in their financial worth but a decrease in their emotional stability. At one point they wonder who I am and what am I doing here.

Movie Stars, Professional Athletes, Television Personalities, Musicians, Recording Artist vs. Business

This is a very difficult comparison. Most people lack the drive and the talent necessary to reach one of these elite jobs. Former Heisman Trophy winner once explained his gridiron success as a commitment to the four D's.

They are: *Desire, Discipline, Dedication, and Determination.*

While the public adoration can be intoxicating and the money plentiful, there is a price to pay. Once an individual becomes a public figure, one's life becomes just that—public. Occasions as simple as dinner or a movie can become logistical nightmares for someone in the public eye. Still, the rewards are well worth the hassles. The financial compensation far outweighs the inconvenience that one may or may not incur. The athletes and performers obviously are worth the money they receive. People constantly complain about how far out of whack the salaries are getting for some of these people just as they pay their money hand over fist.

Yet, they too would be wise to have an established association to protect and secure their rewards.

Sales Representative vs. Business

A sales representative's job simply entails goods and supplies for wholesalers, manufacturers and distributors. Many sales representatives are also paid commission on their sales. The main objective of their job is to maintain present accounts and establish new ones as well. This area of business is known as a salesman's "territory." More than any other profession, a salesperson's success depends directly on his/her performance. The more items one is able to sell, the more lucrative one's job is likely to be. If one's sales are strong, he/she will enjoy good job security and profit from the commission that he/she is able to garner.

A formal education is not usually a requirement. However, some businesses might use a college education as part of their hiring criteria. The ability to persuade people to spend money with your organization is a necessary skill in sales. Whether you acquire it in college or secondary school or you are just born with it is irrelevant. The bottom line is always whether or not one gets the sale.

The average starting salary for a sales representative can vary. Consistent with this profession is a great deal of hours spent working. Aggressive salespeople can work obscene amounts of time. Some work between seventy and eighty hours a week.

The benefits that a salesperson gets are usually considerable. Travel expenses, paid vacations, food stipends and a healthy pension are usually perks that go along with the job. There are some drawbacks to sales too.

Selling is a very hard profession. In addition to extensive travel, the pressure can be extraordinary. Just as great sales can lead to better job security and added commission, poor sales can lead to weak job security and some serious soul searching. Sales representative is a profession with a high turnover rate and low average life expectancy. If one can handle the pressures of the job, it can be lucrative. If one cannot handle the stress that accompanies the immediacy of sales, the job can lead to an early grave.

If one is interested, more knowledge can be obtained by interviews with companies and corporations, and speaking with individuals working in the field. This would be advisable regardless of whichever field of endeavor one chooses.

Politicians vs. Business

Life as a public servant has materialized into one of the best jobs achievable. In addition to impacting the society, one may also earn quite a living. Millions of taxpayers' dollars are spent every year on benefits, offices, staffs with interns and pages, travel, dinner parties, speaking engagements, security and retirement. All of these amenities are afforded to public figures despite the fact that our country has an enormous debt.

If one wanted to examine a model of how <u>not</u> to run a successful business, one needs look no further than the federal government. Congressional efforts to balance the budget have been hysterical. Applying deficit spending to business practice is a sure entrance to the path of destruction not prosperity.

Compare, by December 15, 2010 House of Representatives in session 123 days and Senate 151 days in session (according to Anderson Cooper 360 television show on CNN Dec. 15th at 10 p.m.) over three hundred and fifty plus working days for many hard working people. And compare the benefits and perquisites of legislators with the working person's nil benefits and zero perqs. (perquisites). This isn't a comparison. It is a contrast of magnitude proportions. Remembering one of the more famous politicians saying 'life is not fair"—we know the feeling too well. Life is fair. It's the people in high places that enhance the attitude that life is not fair and then proceed to force it upon others.

In a free enterprise society, few external factors can make a positive difference in sales. If one is struggling with the business, the only alternatives are usually longer hours and/or higher prices on one's merchandise. This tactic should only be employed in times of desperation. It is a long shot to succeed. It usually leads to a larger deficit.

Webster defines the term *deficit* as the amount by which a sum of money falls short of the required or expected amount; thus, a shortage. In business, this practice of spending more money than one takes in is called bankruptcy. It usually leads to the closing of a business due to a collapse in the company's economy. That is also the likely scenario in this country if drastic measures are not taken.

Much of the money garnered from taxes is by the public "sector". Businesses of this nation are the government's principle fund-raisers. Through constant and severe taxation, the federal, state and local governments have been able to capitalize financially on the successful businesses in their area. It is this taxation that serves as the engine that drives the economy. Without the revenue generated from business levies, personal taxes would be astronomically high. Business taxes also serve as the primary supporter of governmental programs, which return nothing to small businesses.

Worse yet, is the yearly raise federal, state and local governments employees get, while people on Social Security sometimes do not get a cost of living raise and have to operate on the same checks that were given the year before. Another case of the rich get richer and the poor are poorer.

Congress does not intentionally discriminate against small business. Their collective interest is to booster the country's economy. If this is at the expense of one particular sector of the economy (i.e. small business), so be it. The result has been unprecedented wealth for some and unmitigated financial decline for others. In the case of small business, it is mostly a take/take relationship on the government's behalf. Overloading small business with a series of tax forms and other bureaucratic weights has led many people to steer clear of what once was considered the 'American Dream'.

Two words that are often confused are deficit and debt. The differences between them are simply the difference between overspending and expenses that are already owed. For example, the United States is operating at a deficit; therefore, it is in debt. In business, one can rarely afford to operate at a loss because the losses (including interest rates) will likely become insurmountable.

The solutions to cutting our nation's debt are quite elementary to point out. Implementing them is an altogether different story though. Downsizing the government, cutting spending and slowing inflation would all help the problem if they could be enacted. The German theorist Max Weber once pointed out; however, the problem with bureaucracy is once it has been created, it is nearly impossible to stop. Arms of the government seem to regenerate themselves each time they are lopped off. Instead of the government shrinking, most statistics point to continued government expansion. This unmitigated growth will continue to facilitate a gap in our deficit and debt will continue to climb.

Real and permanent solutions must be the course of action. Cutting bureaucracy and minimizing the government will cost people jobs. Cuts in defense spending will likely have the same effect. Few politicians are willing to sacrifice their political careers for the betterment of the system. Until more public figures are willing to make such sacrifices, the government will continue to grow, and both the deficit and debt will increase—these are all unpleasant things that new politicians need to address. So, much like retailers the functions put into operation are much like the remedies that businesses on a daily basis tackle.

It is difficult to stay out of debt in a society such as ours. Nearly everything we do is predicated on the idea of debt. It is through assumed debt that banks will grant one a loan. Debt is also a prevailing political theme. Unfortunately, it is debt that will be our undoing if we do not address this problem. In recent years, the government has taken a more corporate approach running itself. This may or may not be a positive move. What is obvious, however, is that the business backbone and energy must be channeled to create a store with little or no debt.

As mentioned, overspending is the cardinal sin in business which leads to bankruptcy. In government, taxes are an easy answer. Small business is afforded no such luxury. Independent business people must not live beyond their means.

Knowing that the money is being misspent may be the hardest obstacle for merchants. Taxes are growing and taxpayer faith is diminishing. This is due to Congress's consistent misuse of money obtained through taxes. The result has been especially hard felt by small business. Many failed small businesses would survive if the government would infuse some commerce back into the business community instead of continually extracting it.

Political discussion and 'town meetings' mean nothing if the solutions proposed are temporary. Solving problems with mirrors can only work for so long before it finally collapses on itself. The problems that face small business now are the same as the ones that have faced us for decades. They will continue for decades more if we lack the courage, foresight and initiative to make real, permanent solutions to this increasingly severe problem.

Small businesses are paying 15.3% for employee Social Security and Medicare. Total cost is 7.65% from employee's paycheck and 7.65% paid by employer. Being a small-business owner in a college town, it breaks my heart to see many of my employees paying out of their respective noses for programs that have a minuté chance of existing when they become old enough to reap the rewards. Many of these students can't even afford a decent meal as they are too busy financing vacations, food, shelter, and other amenities of people who cannot or do not contribute to the economy. Privatization is inappropriate. A few minor changes would be adequate.

Some money never sees its way into the Social Security's considerable pocket. Instead, a Social Security is using the cash influx to strengthen their own position. In essence, by doing nothing, retailers are financing and facilitating their own demise. This must stop for businesses to survive.

Achieving the 'American Dream', the entrepreneur must set up constructive objectives. It is this systematic process of 'life is fair' which makes this dream feasible. Without organization and direction the dream will continue to evolve around a nightmare. Our objective is the 'American Dream' of fair pay for a full day's work. A National Organization of Retailers would be a first and significant step in the correct and infinite direction.

Providing a cure instead of temporary solutions would be the necessary remedy. As technology has set new standards in the way we live, the dysfunctional Congress has not moved with the same momentum. Because of the bi-partisans on issues, there is much ado about nothing; this has stifled the country financially and technically, as well as ethically. Their ability must be contributed to their salaries and ample benefits. With enormous extras, who needs an income? The high economical trend toward technology has moved America to a phenomenon level the likes of which no generation before had the privilege to experience.

Manual Labor vs. Business

Jobs that require manual labor are physically demanding but financially lucrative. One may not make as much money as an engineer, per se, but they are well compensated. This is due in large part to their faith in and the subsequent strength of their respective association. These organizations have taken professions that were once exploited and helped to mold them into political juggernauts. The result has helped many labor oriented professions that are vital to our economy. A final benefit of such a job is that it does not require one to bring it home with them. When their workday is done, they are finished for that day. A small-business owner's life is engulfed in his/her work.

Flight Attendant vs. Business

To be a flight attendant one must be at least 20 years old. Prerequisites include high school diploma or a GED, and completion of two years of post high school education. Attendants must be able to communicate and understand the English language.

They must not exceed a height of 6'2". Flight attendants are required to complete a six and a half-weeks training course costing about $2000.

The perks of a flight attendant include: health insurance, profit sharing, and travel privileges for immediate family after six months. After a certain amount of service travel benefits are extended to friends and other family members. All expenses are paid for during layovers.

APFA (Association of Professional Flight Attendants) provides for their stability and security. Traveling all over the world is an education in itself.

Flight attendants average annual pay starts at $12,800 for beginners and increases up to $40,000 for senior flight attendants. Flight attendants can earn more money by speaking a foreign language and for traveling at night.

Airline Pilot vs. Business

To become an airline pilot one must be at least 21 years of age. Their vision must be corrected to 20/20. They must be tall enough to reach all of the flight controls and their weight must be in proportion to their height. Pilots are also required to complete the necessary ground training and flight training to obtain the necessary ratings (Commercial with an instrument rating, multi-engine or their multi engine Air Transport Pilot Rating). Along with the entire above requirements airline pilots are required to have an FAA first-class medical certificate.

For additional information toll-free numbers can be obtained from many of the companies' respective websites.

Engineering vs. Business

Graduating from college and one year working as an engineer, the new professionals are requested to take an F. E. (Fundamentals of Engineering) test. Upon passing they are admitted into the engineer's association. Their strong organization offers excellent opportunities. Starting pay varies from $35,000-$45,000.

Intelligence in the science of engineering takes a lot of preparation. Studies in this field are very competitive and time consuming. Like everything else it is most satisfying. Most students spent five years in college for an engineering degree, but the rewards are well worth it. Government contracts in this area are plentiful.

Employees vs. Business

Money magazine publishes a list of the 50 hottest jobs in the United States each year. The following are the trends, jobs and salaries of the vocations they have selected in this new millennium.

Due to a lag in time, there will be a variable margin of error depending on the occupation.

Predicted Trends for 2007

1. Careers in computers are very hot.
2. Health care is revving up.
3. Teachers and gum shoes are on a roll.
4. The fastest growing jobs are less and less secure.

If deciding to go into any one of the occupations mentioned below or any of the 13,000 different jobs listed by the Bureau of Labor Statistics, it would be wise to do extensive research concerning <u>all</u> aspects of the job.

A National Organization for Retailers definitely would be a huge asset for any individual starting up a new business. Assistants would enhance small businesses. Working toward any dream takes a lot of determination and energy in order to become successful.

Until there is an association franchises are a good way to go because many of the flaws that plague any business are weeded out. The original individual who started up a franchise usually knows what works and doesn't. Franchisers are extremely talented in picking out the right location. If by chance it's the wrong location, they know when and how to relocate for success.

Franchises offer support and that is essential. Support being one of the most vital superiorities of a National Organization of Retailers is justified. Chain businesses have a good perspective of supply and demand. They are well schooled on how effective new items entered into the establishment will succeed.

In the following predictions of 2007 Published by Money magazine there doesn't seem to be a guide for career, growth and pay for the entrepreneur. The area of small business is too complicated with many levels involved to predict any kind of failure or success. Pay is flexible. Predictions for pay of a self employed person probably cannot be averaged out to any degree because changeability in people's buying habits due to a recession, inflation or a depression. Any kind of assumption would be pure speculation.

Rank	Career	Job Growth (10-yr forecast)
1	Software engineer	46.07%
2	College professor	31.39%
3	Financial advisor	25.92%
4	Human resources manager	23.47%
5	Phyiscian assistant	49.65%
6	Market research analyst	20.19%
7	Computer/IT analyst	36.10%
8	Real estate appraiser	22.78%
9	Pharmacist	24.57%
10	Psychologist	19.14%
11	Advertising manager	20.34%
12	Physical therapist	36.74%
13	Technical writer	23.22%
14	Chiropractor	22.40%
15	Medical scientist	34.06%
16	Physical scientist	12.18%
17	Engineer	13.38%
18	Curriculum developer	27.53%
19	Editor	14.77%
20	Public relations specialist	22.61%
21	Sales manager	19.67%
22	Optometrist	19.73%
23	Property manager	15.30%
24	Actuary	23.16%
25	Writer	17.72%
26	Social service manager	25.52%
27	Paralegal	29.75%
28	Health services manager	22.76%
29	Advertising sales agent	16.33%
30	Physician/Surgeon	23.98%
31	Management analyst	20.12%
32	Occupational therapist	33.61%
33	Mental health counselor	27.18%
34	Landscape architect	19.43%
35	Biotechnology research scientist	17.05%
36	Urban planner	15.17%
37	Lawyer	14.97%
38	Speech-language pathologist	14.57%
39	Meeting and convention planner	22.21%
40	Dietition/Nutritionist	18.30%
41	Biological scientist	17.03%
42	Financial analyst	17.33%
43	Dentist	13.52%
44	Accountant	22.43%
45	Environmental scientist	17.11%
46	Lab technologist	20.53%
47	Registered nurse	29.35%
48	Sales engineer	13.96%
49	Veterinarian	17.39%

A National Organization of Retailers:

Setting up a National Organization of Retailers similar to the structure of the National Education Association, American Medical Association and American Bar Association will be a primary goal. When people think of small business, they rarely associate it with education, medicine or law. That needs to be changed. Public standing and esteem are vital components to our objective.

Issues such as National Health Care, NAFTA and others, consistently go against the collective interest of small business. It is not that the government is against small business. It is simple politics. Elected officials know that having the support of some groups is more advantageous politically and financially than others. Most entrepreneurs cannot compete with Exxon by themselves. Consequently, they receive a virtual slap on the wrist for polluting the Pacific Ocean while we are fined and taxed

Continuously for infractions as minor as mistakenly selling tobacco products to minors or bartender selling ale to an individual under age, the clerk and business are highly penalized. A respected and united organization would curtail this phenomenon. Instead of the government monitoring and controlling our every action, it would be the independent business owners who would help influence the government.

If there has ever been any pro small business issues passed by Congress, then I failed to have experienced it. The small business economy is suffering from taxpayer's money being geared toward education in the form of enterprises on state property competing with our small establishments. Colleges of higher learning in America have become financial institutions while the student's tuition, room and board fees are skyrocketing every year.

When tax money is allocated to education it seems to take on a whole new meaning. Could this be deception? Makes one wonder where and if there were ever any ethics. And, yet there is an ethics course being taught. How can that be? Can one really row a boat up and down stream at the same time?

Maybe the American Dream has taken on a different perspective in the form that everyone works for the government while private enterprise is no longer feasible. That can't be right unless our ideal capitalistic economy has taken on a new unpleasant structure.

A reality check is in order. How can small businesses with all their expenditures compete with businesses on state property that have low expenses compared to expenses of independent business people? If businesses on state property over extend themselves, again the government bails them out with our hard earned tax money.

This conclusion should help you better understand which area is better. Are the rewards of working for someone else better than working for you with no guarantees or perks? This leads to **Employee vs. Employer**.

Millions opt to pursue other endeavors when they felt their dreams of entrepreneurial ship would not materialize. Nothing is wrong with that. They understood their limitations of dream fulfillment. It's not for others to analyze. An example of dreams not fulfilled is television's "American Idol". Out of a hundred thousand would-be singers, only a few dreams were fulfilled along with the one American Idol left standing.

Three men overcoming tremendous odds: According to their stories on television's "The Big Idea", they all hit rock bottom and took advantage of America's opportunities while side stepping adversities.

1) The self made billionaire Paul Orfalea, businessman, visionary and philanthropist, homeless at an early age developed Kinko's and sold to federal express for billions. Great faith in family and friends helped his drive to the top.

Read his book, "Copy This", if interested in learning more. He is now giving back by helping the homeless. He represents an excellent example why capitalism is good and greed sucks. May God bless? A great Samaritan the world can be proud of. He cares.

2) Ron Meyer, school drop out to Hollywood Titans. He is President and Chief Operations Officer of Universal Studios. Ron is co-founder of Creative Artists Agency in 1975. Involved with the careers of Cher, Streisand, Cruise, Hanks and Madonna produced "American Pie", and many other top movies.

3) Jeff Henderson is head chef at the Café Baggio in Las Vegas due to his culinary skills. Learn more about this family man by reading his

book, "Cooked": from the streets to the stove—from cocaine to Foie Gras.

Accenting the positive and eliminating the negative is what these three men did to overcome. They focused on the future and did not let the past determine their destiny. All three men made gigantic positives from failures.

Two ladies who had the staminate and fulfilled their dreams are 1) Jennifer Hudson, the American Idol voted out in seventh place, overcame a judge's remark "If you don't win, you'll never be heard or seen again" spoken to her backstage after she lost idol. Two years later won an Oscar and Golden Globe for her first role in a movie, "Dreamgirls". The beat goes on. Adversity didn't and won't hold her back. Her professional future gets brighter and brighter. America loves her.

2) Heather Mills competing in "Dancing with the Stars." has a fake leg. Her determination won. Although she didn't win the trophy, she fulfilled her dream by competing on the show finishing in the middle of the pack. That is an achievement.

Very few attain their dream, but these five found it by eliminating the past and all its obstacles, capability, talent, perseverance and <u>never giving up.</u>

Remedy

+

Repetition

=

Reward

United We Stand: Now the cup runniest over—less risk—more confidence—enjoyment—happiness—innovation—knowledge—

respect—understanding—vision—better attitude—change ability—competence personification—**restored ethics**—promotes capitalism while eliminating super capitalism known as greed—honesty—integrity—no tax harassments—a political powerhouse—family 24/7—and support.

Uniting is the only stimulus package small business needs for our family 24/7 and business. To quote our President Barack Obama, "Yes, we can." The strength would be phenomenal. Quoting our President again, "Yes we did."

An owner of small business cannot do it alone, as a network of people is necessary to move this mountain. You're invited to the best party in town.

2009 stimulus package gives money to the rich and the poor a tax break. What? Why doesn't the poor businessperson get a financial package? Again we are doing the highly improbable rowing the boat up and down water at the same time.

We've got to organize to get where we need to go. Mismanagement in corporation gets rewards. Something is wrong, but what? Is it that our government has disrespect for small business? I think so. I've experience many years of mistreatment by our government with their vindictive ways. Our motto: Remedy + Repetition = Reward.

Change for small business—unite. Every politician wants to move small business further to the background. Our failure to unite enhances their leverage.

CHAPTER 4

GETTING STARTED FINANCIALLY

Adequate working capital is essential to become successful in business. Regardless of what one starts with financially, chances are some money will be borrowed. In the beginning the three main sources of income for an investment would be cash, loans and credit.

Beginning resources:
1. Cash—Money individual has on hand for investment
2. Loans—Borrowed money
3. Credit—Charged purchases

Other possible sources for accumulating money are family, friends, and grants by the government.

Loans:
Most loans come via the banking industry. It is not always easy to get a low interest loan from the bank. The most common loan in this situation is the commercial loan—prime rate plus an additional three percent.

The minute the business loan is processed and the papers signed, the company has incurred a debt.

Another option in securing a bank loan is if one has a co-signer. When one does opt to co-sign for someone else, it is imperative co-signers understand that they will burden the debt if the primary signer fails to meet the terms of his/her agreement with the bank.

Perks:

While some professions are laden with incentives and perks, others must scratch and claw their way to success. For example, many business jobs allow their employees to travel throughout the world at the company's expense. These trips include meals, lodging and other expenses. However, these excursions are well worth it to the company financing the trip. Multi-million dollar accounts are worth a few thousand dollars to larger corporations. In stark contrast, the entrepreneur often must struggle just to pay the bills.

Property:

Another common question pertains to the actual cost of funding a business. Businesses are like the people who run them—each different from the rest. The cost of the business building or leasing a building is essential to the success of the profit in the business.

Location:

More importantly would be the location of the business as to the cost value of the rent. This factor is crucial because location is of the key to the success of many businesses.

The best way to go today would be to purchase the property. In fact, the property appreciation may be more profitable than the business itself. All the repairs and new beautification made by the tenant increase the value of the property. Added value could be a detriment for the renter when signing a new lease. Many places do not have rent control; therefore, if renting, once the lease has expired the landlord may double or triple the rent.

One of my five brothers, William bought property priced at $250,000 in downtown Columbus, Ohio for his law firm. A year later the same property was reevaluated at $1.4 million. This is concrete proof that owning one's own business building is an excellent asset. For those who choose to buy the building, the space owner is also responsible for all the repairs, property taxes and insurance. However, in the past few years many people have been unable to make mortgage payments. Millions of people are faced with property foreclosures

Taxes:

Taxes are another factor. Although this comes under payroll, retailers must understand that they have to equal the amount of Social Security and Medicare paid to the government deducted from each employee's paycheck along with other tax regulation set by the federal, state and local government.

Insurance:

Perhaps the most important financial aspect of a business comes with its insurance. Liability, fire, theft etc. are the types of insurance usually extended to a business. As most things go up from year to year so does the insurance.

Utilities:

Before the business can be opened, agreements must be met with the local utility companies. As each utility company is visited, forms will have to be filled out to establish an account with promises to pay. These companies usually require a retainer fee. Another bureaucratic step comes when one has to purchase his/her vendor's license. These licenses are usually inexpensive and require minimal paper work.

To reach each destination requires quite a bit of legwork, though. It is quite surprising to many people as to how much running around and paper work must be completed at each agency just to take care of things as basic as light and heat. It can be quite a long process. It is often the little things that become so important for the big picture. Though many papers must be completed and retainer fees deposited, these are necessary steps that pave the way for a successful business.

Merchandise:

The next step deals with the merchandise. It is the merchandise that one opts to carry that will serve as the lifeline of one's company. This may be the most tedious part of the entire process. Perhaps this is because there are no shortcuts. Wholesale catalogs must be obtained and utilized. These catalogs bare the names, phone numbers and addresses of the companies. One can find these information packets in a myriad of places including: computers via the Internet, friends, sales associates, advertisements, libraries, brochures and the local telephone directory.

Credit References:

Each company, wholesaler or manufacturer will explain the firm's credit policies to any retailer. Cash before delivery, cash on delivery or a delayed payment are all types of credit arrangements typically made between retailers and distributors. Many firms require cash for merchandise. If a firm does not extend credit and the retailer does not meet his/her payment on time, a monthly finance charge is normally assessed. This serves to drive the borrower further in debt.

The person in small enterprise will have to establish credit by issuing references to suppliers. References should include local banks where items were financed, such as: home, car, appliance etc. One's punctuality in paying off these items is usually a good measuring stick as to how well he/she will meet payment deadlines on the business loan. Assuming the previous payments have been met on time, the bank should issue the prospective loaner a good credit rating to any inquirers. Department stores and credit card companies may also serve as good references.

If the business is able to take root and grow, past suppliers may also be added to one's list of references. Once the report is full enough, a shopkeeper may apply for a rating with a large firm like Dun & Bradstreet. As a highly respected company, D. & B. specializes in issuing credit ratings for businesses. Their rating is two-fold and consists of (1.) the minimum amount of credit a supplier can safely allow the merchant and (2.) the person's timely ability to pay for merchandise.

To gain acceptance to a company such as Dun & Bradstreet, one must fill out a questionnaire regarding company facts like: the company's name, address, phone number, web-site, owner's name, number of employees, annual sales, balance sheet (a list of assets and liabilities), net worth, banking institutions and other business constituents. To gain a favorable rating from one of these companies can serve as a huge advantage to a small business. For more information on Dun & Bradstreet write them at:

Dun & Bradstreet
Information Resources
Department 178
One Imperial Way

Allentown, PA 18195-0010

A positive rating by such a company will help to speed up transactions by giving possible lenders a quick and reliable barometer of how likely a person is to pay back their debt. After D. & B. compiles all information necessary, they will issue a store rating. Again, the two parts are:

1. The minimum amount of credit a supplier can safely allow the merchant
2. The ability the business person has to pay for merchandise from the suppliers: slow, on time, or quick.

These companies utilize the information that the small business supplies to them as well as the reports from distributors that the business has worked with to help to formulate its' rating. One bad experience with just one supplier may hurt the rating of an otherwise competent and responsible retailer; however, it's highly unlikely. For this reason, it is paramount that one be diplomatic as well as pragmatic when one is running his/her business.

Perspective:

In business, one learns early that what is the norm today may be the exception tomorrow and vice versa. For this reason, it is of utmost importance to run one's business with reverence for yesterday but an eye on tomorrow. Change is a natural part of evolution. While the business grows and expands, so too will its problems provided one does not change with the times and the establishment.

As businesses grow, they require more help to accommodate their expansion. This creates jobs for the economy. By constantly taxing businesses, financing that could be spent on creating jobs instead goes to paying off increasing debt. President John F. Kennedy understood this all too well. He reduced the percentage of taxpayer's federal income tax. Bill was later signed into law under President L. B. Johnson in 1964.

Increased supporting of all business across the board gave companies a chance to better financial status. President George W. Bush in the new millennium has taken a tax cut approach. However, his tax cut was limited by Congress, and may not be enough to curb a recession. It was too little—too late. Recession occurred in 2008. Congress has a spending addiction and should seek help by attending a Spending Addiction Rehab before it's too late. If they don't quit spending, this country will suffer a deep depression. A change not needed.

Change:

Change is something all small businesses must accept and plan for. Both internal and external changes will occur and woe is one who is unprepared. Change adjustment is vital. In addition to constant government sanctions are the changing climate and whims of American shoppers. These are just some of the factors retailers need to handle.

Accounting:

All account records must be done on a daily basis. Bookkeeping is not permitted to lag behind. If a tax form is not submitted timely and correctly, penalties almost always follow. A mistake of any kind may result in a costly fine. Sales tax in Ohio has to be filed and mailed with a monthly check within 21 days of the following month, and due in the Department of Taxation by the 23rd of the month.

The next chapter is devoted to an explanation of every tax form that the federal, state and local governments require; thus, only one reason the expenses cannot be accurately recorded.

There are always letters addressed to the business of an expense that was unexpected. No way to record a detail of each and every unknown debt until it occurs.

All businesses incur more expenses than expected:

To accurately forecast all future expenses is difficult. It is critical for the entrepreneur to make room in his/her budget for these hidden costs. Even the most intimate knowledge and familiarity with past fees such as: rent, phone, electric, gas and all maintenance will not guarantee one will be able to predict future costs. Past trends are no longer applicable.

A building that rented for $100 a month in 1968 may go for as much as $1000 or more, today and $2000 or $3000 shortly thereafter.

It was in the last few years of the 1990's that rent really skyrocketed. It is all too common for leases to increase by as much as 200% without reason. Landlords justify this practice explaining that they have to do something to help control their spiraling costs and levies. With local, state and federal governments consistently sticking their hands in the cookie jar, it is only a matter of time before the jar runs empty unless the profit margin is inflated.

Estimations of future costs are futile because there are so many determinants. Other expenses that one might encounter may include supplies, materials and other necessities such as: painted signs, neon lights, or otherwise, brooms, carpeting, vacuums, vacuum bags, cleanser, cups, desk blotters, erasers, stapler, staples, computer paper, ink cartridge, clocks, flashlights, cabinets, shelves, fans, ledgers, light bulbs, locks, medical supplies, mirrors, mops, paint, paint supplies, all paper supplies used in office or throughout the store, paperclips, paper towels, pens, rags, rubber bands, scrub buckets, soap, thumb tacks, tissues, tool kit, towels, trash cans, wall decorations, wax for tiled or hardwood floors, bags for purchases, window supplies, continuous purchase of restroom supplies, flashlights, batteries, register tape, coffee, coffee filters, envelopes for mailing, stationery, bank charges for accounts, checks, deposit slips, daily deposits and overdrafts may all add to a business' expenses.

There are also expenses that are not monthly. They may include equipment, fixtures, office furniture, registers, desks, shelving, chairs, lamps, adding machines, copiers, computers and their stands. Other considerations include: fire extinguishers, snow shovels, ice salt and any other maintenance or cleaning supplies.

Considering the type of retail store an entrepreneur would like to pursue, be prudent when making out a complete list of everything needed. List how often items are repeated. If one mails one hundred letters a month, the average cost to the business would be $44 dollars in stamps. Over the course of a year, this price would amount to $528. Little items can become quite expensive in the long term.

Stores:
The types of purchases one makes will directly depend on which type of retail store one plans to operate. A restaurant, for example,

will require such things as refrigerators, stoves, grills, ovens, working counters, stools, walk-in coolers, soda fountain bar, eating area, booths, clothing for employees, utensils, menus, tables and chairs. There are also some less obvious expenses involved like napkin holders, napkins, ash trays, toothpicks, assorted dishes and of course an assortment of containers for food to eat inside or for carry outs. If one decides to add delivery service as well, he/she may have to cover the costs of the delivery cars, the gasoline, the maintenance and the parking. In conjunction with each other, these expenses can become quite formidable.

Appliance and electronics stores are run completely different. Therefore their needs and fears are distinct. One need for these types of stores that most people would not initially consider is that of many electrical outlets. Without the sufficient number of outlets, the business will be unable to showcase many of its products. Also, critical to the entrepreneur of this field are delivery trucks and a competent repair service. All businesses incur more expenses than expected.

Ice cream parlors will require freezers, scoops, dishes, cups, napkins, plastic utensils, food containers, eating area and the product itself. Regardless of the business, the list of needs and accessories is seemingly endless.

Travel lodging is a unique business. After the property is purchased, one must deal with land upkeep, parking facilities, overhead signs and highway access. The office, lounge, dining area, hallways and swimming area all have to be furnished with the needs of each section. There is a lot more to a hotel than just its rooms, although that is where the average customer is likely to spend most of his/her time. The beds, chairs, desks, stands, lamps, closet items, bedding, decorations, curtains, restroom supplies, telephone, television set, coffee maker, air conditioner, computer, heating and adequate plumbing are all on the list of expenses.

Issues such as linens are important. Laundry must be cleaned on a daily basis. In most motels, there will be several washers and dryers within it. Incidental items such as pens, writing paper, soap, towels (bath, hand, floor mats etc.) all have a way of leaving the hotel without detection. That's why so many hotels/motels have their name all over these items. Though they might be stolen, these items can serve as wonderful advertisements. The more decorative the items, the more inviting they become too would be pilferers. Missing items must be replaced before the next guests check in. Another expense in travel lodges is with security. Inside locks as well as outside locks are as essential for protection as they are for guest comfort. Patio furniture is another potential cost to the travel care entrepreneur. Furniture must be both durable and comfortable.

The room is only one phase of the motel, but a small portion of the financial structure of the business. Much of the real cost and profit come from exterior concerns like aesthetic and customer accommodations. The owner of a small motel has a rougher time than the entrepreneur of larger motels. Large chains are able to buy in bulk. This mass type of ordering allows them to enjoy tremendous discounts. However, motel ownership retrieves their investments by its costly charge for rooms per night. There are many hotel and motel management courses offered that more thoroughly outline this specialized field.

Then there are luxuries if affordable such as: a kitchen and all its appliances, employees' dining and conference room plus all the necessary furniture, cook ware, eating utensils and television (cable) are items that an owner of a small business is personally responsible for. It is also important for the aspiring entrepreneur to remember we are living in a fitness age. More and more businesses are installing weight rooms, spas, showers etc. to accommodate their employees.

When considering any small business, expenditures must likewise be pondered. Although the regulations and requirements are fairly similar for all business ventures, some businesses require a bit more analysis than others. Just seeking out a location requires a great deal of time, diplomacy, energy, patience and money.

The new retail owner will have to make up a complete agenda of supplies needed to help his/her business. This can only be found by doing bona fide research into one's prospective endeavor.

Owning rental property can be an excellent opportunity, especially in today's world where rent is outlandish. If one does choose to purchase property for the purposes of later leasing it, they should seriously consider retaining a legal consultant. (Contracts are legal documents that signify agreement by two or more parties.) One's leasing agreement must follow contemporary state law.

Some businesses do nothing but rent out homes and apartments. Many of these enterprises are legal firms. These firms often have their own maintenance crews, legal consultation, accounting staffs etc. The advantage of this type of business is its ability to cater to a myriad of needs. The prevailing criticism of it is its impersonal nature. The larger the firm, the less likely one is to be able to interact with each other on a personal basis.

Independent people who have rentals know the advantage of the high cost of rent and the way it raises. Buying property and dividing it into sleeping and study rooms has made millionaires for many. Rental property is a booming business, but not in today's recession/depression.

The most important thing to remember for the entrepreneur is that the business is theirs. The success of the business ultimately rests on his/her shoulders. The business owner is the company, and must be well organized to enjoy success. Lists may be tedious, but they can also serve as a business owner's best friend. Small items can cut well into business profits

Projecting into the future about the laws of economics, owners of small business must consider the inflation cycle. All costs for running an enterprise are taken from the owner's initial profit; therefore, the raise in the costs of supplies, maintenance and repairs are cause for a lower personal profit.

The Focus of this book is small business:

We have focused almost primarily on the art of small business. There may come a day when one decides to make the leap into big business. Of course, this is always a possibility, but unfortunately it is not the focus of this book. There are some similarities between big and small business, however. A self-employed person of a small business is essentially the same job as a C.E O. of a larger company. A striking difference is that most small business ventures don't have a board of directors, and large corporations have for labor and management the benefits that a national retailers association can provide.

An owner of a small business is responsible for most of the following comprehensive itemization of the expenditures. Once becoming a retailer, you be the judge as to who is spending your money.

Summary—The expenditures:

1. Rent
2. Electric
3. Gas
4. Water
5. Sewer
6. Garbage
7. Telephone
8. Materials
9. Postage
10. Stationery
11. Tax penalties and interest on bookkeeping mistakes or late filing
12. Payroll staff, clerks, janitors, office, and many other types of employees
13. Attorneys or legal advice if a legal matter is involved
14. Supplies
15. Repairs
16. Bags for merchandise
17. Tools
18. Food appliances and supplies
19. Licenses
20. Advertisement
21. Equipment
22. Fixtures
23. Incidentals
24. Bookkeeper or CPA
25. Car expenses
26. Freight on merchandise
27. Bank service charges
28. Bank costs for checking account, including checks, deposit slips, deposits & bank bags
29. Insurance
30. Electrician
31. Plumber
32. Volunteering costs, such as charitable organizations or merchandise given for benefits

33. Seasonal window decorations
34. Seasonal store decorations
35. Monthly finance charge on past due bills
36. Debts from suppliers
37. Educational material for reading and studying—or courses of study
38. Business literature
39. Bad check written by customers
40. Goods lost to shoplifters
41. Workers' compensation
42. Bureau of employment services
43. FUTA—federal unemployment tax association
44. 7.65% employee's payroll for social security and Medicare (employees Social Security and Medicare tax amount equaled by employer)
45. Parking accommodations
46. Percentage of sales paid to banks for accepting credit and debit cards—plus payment for the machine and sales receipt tape.

Payroll:

Employees will be needed to help run the business. The employer must not only manage his/her own finances, but they must also document and pay the employees' wages, taxes, unemployment tax and worker's compensation as well. A few years ago, there was a law passed known as the Paper Reduction Act. This "reduction" has managed to triple the amount of paperwork required of small businesses. In my many years in business no law has ever been passed to reduce unnecessary administrative processes. Instead, the tedious nature of taxes has grown with each passing year.

When a book requires studying just to fill out the accompanying tax sheet, the task can be quite complicated. Tax departments are forever reorganizing themselves and their modus operandi. For this reason, it may be advisable for the aspiring small-business owner to hire a Certified Public Accountant to help manage one's resources.

The average employee pays 15.3% in Social Security. The employee is only directly responsible for 7.65%, burdening the employer with the other half of the levy. Other payroll expenses include Federal Income

Tax, Workers' Compensation, Welfare Services, Employment Services and the Federal Unemployment Tax Association. With the increasing amount of such agencies, the government is taking more and more money out of the average person's paycheck. This type of pyramid financing scheme cannot sustain itself on a national level.

Shoplifting

Another important factor for small business is the management and reduction of shoplifting. Anytime there is merchandise involved, there will be a presence of pilfering. Thievery falls into three different categories: employee theft, company theft and customer theft. The premise that most people are honest allows the few dishonest to take advantage of the system.

Of the many customers that shop in one's store daily, perhaps only a few people are there to steal. All store employees must keep an eye on every customer. Sometimes the most pristine and distinguished looking people can make the savviest thieves.

Plain clothed employees may help a business. People are far more likely to steal in front of other customers than they are employees of the store. A plain clothed employee may be more likely to catch the criminal in the act. Don't be afraid to approach all customers. Approaching a customer serves as a dual purpose. It increases the level of interaction between the customer and the shopkeeper and is a likely deterrent to any would-be-shoplifters.

It is important to realize that knowing one's customers does not necessarily excuse them from stealing. There have been many businesses that have been robbed by people who knew the owner's daily schedule. Thieves have to be masters of deception to succeed. Almost everything they appear to be doing is actually a diversion from their objective. They may work alone or with others. Regardless of their style, it is pivotal to remember they are attempting to trick the shopkeeper. It is imperative for the life of the business to prohibit this from happening while at the same time maintaining the diplomacy and temperance that all legitimate customers expect and deserve.

Employee Honesty

The employee can dramatically affect the profit and/or deficit of a business. Some polls have shown that as much as 80% of all company thieves are internal. Employees have access to nearly all areas of a business. This can make them great assets or dangerous interlopers. Thus it is essential that the employer keep the employees satisfied at all times.

Employee theft is a very serious offense that can and should not be tolerated. It is a violation that breaks a very deep trust. Perhaps, at least in the past, only marriage and family relied more heavily on trust. When that trust is broken, the relationship must be severed. Without trust, the situation can only grow uncomfortable. It can also destroy the morale of a business.

One major advantage of a small business comes with its inventory. The smaller volume of stock allows the storeowner to keep more precise records of what he/she has and how much money it is likely to garner. Even a slight deviation will clue the business owner in on a possible theft. If this deviation is happening consistently, it is likely that an employee is causing the problem. Thus, anything taken becomes a business liability.

Bad Checks

Any business that accepts bank vouchers as credit runs the risk of pay fraud. There will be times in the life of any business that someone will pass on to one's store a phony check. Like the customer/shoplifter relationship, it is very difficult to discern between the bad check and the legitimate one. Perhaps the worst part of the whole deal is that one does not realize that they have accepted an illegitimate check until their bank processes it.

Experienced check forgers may have sophisticated methods to help carry out their crime. Perhaps the most common of these are the use of false identification cards. These cards may give the unsuspecting retailer a false sense of security about the legitimacy of the customer. There are some measures that a retailer can take to curb this problem. Unfortunately, most of them are too consuming of time and money to be useful to the owner of a small business.

If a check does not meet the requirements of the bank due to insufficient funds, this is called check bouncing. If a check does bounce, the balance of it plus an additional service fee are subtracted from the business' account at the bank. This can cause the shoestring budget of the small business a great deal of problems.

A surprisingly high percentage of people write bad checks unintentionally. For this reason, they are very accommodating about repaying their check. They are also responsible for the financial penalty. In the cases that the faulty check was written intentionally, it is nearly improbable to track them down.

Banks

Dealing with banks is sometimes like a tragic/comedy situation. Review the situation—many banks charge their customers for things such as: bank bags with their name on them (free advertisement for the banks), charge interest on loans, only give loans when there is more than enough collateral, charge your account if you have an overdraft, charge your account for each customer check that bounces, charge huge amounts for check books, check book cover, a charge for deposit slips, service charge for just having an account with the bank and the list goes on.

There is tremendous overhead for the business when dealing with the banks. The comedy is they charge you for everything; thus, having you think they are doing you a favor. We need satisfaction, and a N.O.R. (National Organization of Retailers) would be highly qualified to achieve this goal by having banks within the association. We need solutions not problems. However, banks must meet their obligations also.

In Summary

Running a business of any size can be far more involved emotionally and economically than most people can fathom. Always remember the importance of working capital. Without a strong financial base, the business cannot succeed. Capitalism's greatest strength and weakness may be its ambiguity. This is never more true than when deciding how and what to spend on one's business; thus the owner must spend the working capital wisely.

America is forever growing and prospering. This is in large part due to the success of many businesses that have contributed to propel our land forward. All businesses are like roller coasters. They are always moving with a series of dips and twists. If the entrepreneur makes a commitment to running his/her business ethically and pragmatically, he/she is virtually guaranteed to experience far more peaks than valleys.

We have reached a stage in our development that we must address. The future success calls for the litany of small business that sprinkles this nation to join forces and become one. A united and directed organization would help small business far more profoundly than any outside organization ever would or could.

Before the recession we were told these are good times in America. Astute owners of small business were suffering their worst time ever because their voices are not heard and answers will not surface until an association is established. The times are negative, but I have strong positive beliefs that owners of small businesses will pull themselves up by the boot straps and trail blaze the road to optimism; an optimism of everlasting peace, prosperity and progress by conquering all the obstacles and adversaries with teamwork.

As our two-party system in Congress blames one another for their shortcomings, small business rationalizes by accusing the government for their success or failure. However, we are not meant to blame. Pointing out this fact is necessary so we'll be responsible to rectify each problem, and not hold others responsible. Therefore solutions must be developed and carried out.

An ideal motto: <u>REMEDY + REPETITION = REWARD</u>

A short research study would be helpful and involves:

1. Capital: An extensive study is important. The correct amount of money needed should not be underestimated. The stakes are far too high to cut corners financially.
2. Type of Business: For example, retail merchandising or selling food and beverages are a few of numerous businesses.
3. Market Size: Number of people drawn to the area. Who buys? What do customers purchase? When do they buy? How can a business attract more customers? How can a store get customers to buy more?

4. Potential Expansion: Expansion is only possible if there is sufficient room and capital to accommodate the move.

5. Location: Select a prime location for your establishment. Capital and Location are top priorities for success.

6. Business hours/family: Business owners are in the unique position of determining their own hours provided everything goes as planned. That means that we can choose to spend more time with our families. We cannot do this without financial repercussion, however. A society that makes one choose between an intimate family and a financially stable one is hard for survival. This needs changed. In many areas of Europe people are given two hour lunch periods; thus, the evening is spent with family. In America several TV shows, have been known to bring some families together in the same room.

7. Managing Change: We must envision the future through effective innovations, communications, compassion, flexibility and preparation of a common goal along with optimizing competent strategies in the use of technology. It is up to us to make this metamorphosis in retail management. Constantly learning new discoveries in technology adds to a manager's versatility to change.

8. Experience: This is critical in helping to develop a clear and concise strategy. Therefore, it would be helpful to seek out the experience of some owners of small business and add to one's present knowledge. Positive direction is rewarding. My dad once said, "You have the knowledge, now you must experience." In other words, what is knowledge worth if not put into practice? Follow your dream.

9. Image: The new entrepreneur's ability to achieve a successful environment with a constructive image depends on one's ability to create customer satisfaction by quickly making prudent decisions and delegating authority. The key is personnel management—hiring competent and honest employees.

10. Supply and Demand: Goods readily available on demand are extremely necessary or customers will go elsewhere; thus, the sale is lost.

11. Minimum Wage Problem: Increased minimum wage may bugle the paycheck but the taxes are higher and the consumer's purchasing power is less. Decreased taxes increase the paycheck and buying power. Giving the employee the proper check cannot be done if everyone is paid the same.

12. Taxes: It is a cliché for a person to complain about taxes. In fact, these complaints have become as much an institution as the taxes themselves. Clichés exist for a reason. For every second that your business is open, Uncle Sam is dipping into your cash register. He is not alone. State and local governments are standing in line like vultures trying to seize whatever loose change one might have. With all these governmental fat cats pillaging what they can, it is the owners of small businesses who suffer. That brings us to our first of several diatribes.

13. Profit Margin: This is the amount of profit made on the goods by subtracting the wholesale price from the retail price. There will be variables, such as: one item you sell for ten dollars may cost a different wholesale price than another piece of merchandise sold for ten dollars.

14. Prepare and maintain a budget: keep track of money collected and its allocation, record keeping including payroll, the banking process (deposits, credit card purchases and maintenance, calculating discrepancies, methods of inventory control, purchasing merchandise and compare prices of goods.

15. Knowledge: Gain all the information available and apply as needed in job responsibilities, analyze and do research work, arrange working schedule, study communications and personal relations to interact with others, perform all your duties to the best of your ability by applying all the knowledge you learn in your market research evaluation. Prioritizing all ideas and implementing them will provide one with the education for entrepreneurial success.

The role of an entrepreneur:
1. Competency
The ability to function effectively and efficiently within the framework of a healthy business is necessary for success. Important

tools are knowledge and experience, along with excellent ethics, hard work and honesty, for a confident retailer.

2. Managerial Process

The leadership supervisor is responsible for all the operations of the business.

The manager/supervisor must motivate others by constantly being subjective as to suggestions that are of value to the business.

3. Money Control

A budget has to be maintained efficiently and effectively by keeping accurate records of the sales and spending within the company. Many expenses were explained in this chapter, but each manager will have to provide for his/her specialized retailing functions. Inventory and sales must be outlined, maintained and overseen on a daily basis along with any noticeable shortages. A discrepancy must be dealt with so on the next day no losses are repeated and corrections materialize.

4. Innovation

Be able to present new strategies and ideas as the economy changes. Help the business to change as your competition enters or leaves the market. The owner must have the capability to improve the business' performance on a daily basis.

5. Communications

Retailer must takes responsibility for overall interaction between employees and customers by seeing that pure and honest relationships are ethical and acceptable. Respect others by showing a willingness to use their ideas subjectively, and provide a friendly atmosphere to accomplish major goals.

The ability to know the difference of constructive communication is vital. The capacity to function with others on even terms without the overuse of authority provides for the comfort of an expanding business. Careful and effective leaders do not 'deviate from the norm' or conventions of society by stepping on another to improve or for the betterment of their goals. Many times an owner over expands and that, my friend, is where the trouble begins. Listen to others input.

6. Honesty is foremost

It is not all diplomacy and tact when dealing with honesty in every situation. The feelings of others must be considered with integrity, compassion and understanding, regardless of status within the company.

7. Risks and Changes

Risk and change are two components that affect the business and must be researched occasionally. Adapting methods to meet new challenges must be addressed and implemented as to the direction and focus of the establishment.

One must understand the risks in the business landscape. Working together in honesty to accomplish the goals on friendly terms will instill competence and confidence. Open communications for suggestions will help when involved in many of the new risks and changes that may occur.

Remedy + Repetition = Reward.

The solutions need to be created before the problems occur. Seeking out a way to solve instead of pondering the same old problems will enhance and accomplish the goals at a faster pace with less confusion. One must use all of his/her knowledge and experience for solving each problem. This leads to financing your business successfully.

Congressman Don Manzullo—Illinois—Chairman of the House Small Business Committee is from a small-business family. His family has been in business since 1963, and the congressman has been a representative for twelve years. It appeared he may create some good for small business. Didn't happen.

His intentions were noble. He believes that the biggest threats to small enterprise are taxes, regulatory relief and government interference with the market. It is not known how he planned to accomplish his goals; however, doing something constructive for small business is a step in the right direction.

Representative Nydia Velazquez—N.Y.—who, in 2007, holds the position may be able to push for pro small business issues more effectively. Although I'm not looking forward to anything positive that businesspeople can relate to.

CHAPTER 5

TAXES, TAXES, TAXES UP, UP AND AWAY— GOVERNMENT CONTROL

We have reached a period in our nation's development where many of the laws and regulations that once served as the strings that tied this confederacy together are no longer consistent with the will of the people. This has resulted in greater friction and mistrust between America's government and its citizens than ever before. Some states still have laws in their books that prohibit certain types of romantic interludes that a married couple may indulge in. In Pennsylvania, for example, sorority houses are illegal. It was once believed that these houses were actually incognito brothels. The most obvious example of dated laws may be with our current tax codes.

German writer Max Weber once said that bureaucracy's greatest problem was that once it was set into motion, there was no way of stopping it. He was criticizing his own government at the time, but his point is ageless. Too many times in recent history, our government's solution to bad tax laws has been additional taxes. Does that make sense to anyone? Tax after tax after tax has been introduced to correct the imbalance created by the preceding levies. This is exactly what Mr. Weber was criticizing.

The quick fix mentality of our lawmakers requires immediate gratification. If one area shows considerable improvement while all of the others show a moderate decline, a crafty politician will consider this "progress." Another trick that they often use is with a budget "cut."

Politicians will call anything that doesn't cost as much as they projected a "cut." Imagine if your local grocery store raised the price of steak by one dollar a month. In June, the steak costs six dollars; in July, that figure grows to seven dollars; In August, the cost of the steak jumps to eight dollars, and so on. If in September, the grocery store charged $8.50 for the steak, would you consider that a price cut? This type of mentality is exactly what is facing American taxpayers.

Our government rules by consensus. Consequently, instead of choosing one option over another, lawmakers simply take the path of least resistance. Unfortunately, for owners of small businesses that path almost always leads directly into the pocketbooks of America's middle class. With such a large and capable financial base, it has been the middle class who has been charged the most to help finance our nation.

Time and taxes have now whittled down this once huge segment of our population. The gap between the rich and the poor may have never been as apparent as it is today. Lawmakers may finally be forced into decisions that they have been so reluctant to make for generations. When faced with the responsibility of choosing between the politicians' financiers and a class that has never voted, the decision will be easy, if not reprehensible. This means that the time is now for small business to stratify together, and form an association with a. To borrow a very famous quotation from British poet, Lord Bryon, "He who hesitates is lost." The window of opportunity has been opened. If small business fails to act quickly and decisively, it is small enterprise losing the most.

The following scenario is an explanation of all the present taxes and tax forms that the person in small business is required to fill out and mail. A check for the balance due is required. This has to be done by specific time to avoid an assessment—penalty plus interest charges. The tax work requires hours of bookwork, an envelope for mailing and a postage stamp for each item. Here is a brief summary of the pay free bookwork the business people are to complete for the government.

1. At the end of every quarter, a quarterly tax form is required to be completed within 30 days. This form is called the *Employers' Quarterly Federal Tax Return*. These returns are

due or postmarked no later than January 31, April 30, July 31 and October 31.One must read all tax forms very carefully. Some tax forms are required to be in the tax office on the last day instead of postmarked on the last day of the month.

The *Employers' Quarterly Federal Tax Return* form includes the number of employees for the quarter; the total amount paid all employees, total Income Tax, Social Security and Medicare of the collective group. This makes a total of 7.65% from the employee and 7.65% from the employer. This makes a total l5.3% in Social Security and Medicare.

In essence, the employer is unwittingly paying l5.3% of the money earned to the government. If anyone were to take 15.3% of their paycheck and invest it conservatively, chances are they would earn less than the government established Social Security and Medicare benefits. Of course, there is the possibility of losing it all.

Many people old enough to collect Social Security checks invested them in Lucent Technologies only to see almost all of it disappear by the year 2001. Privatizing Social Security could be disastrous.

There is a penalty and interest charge if the total amount due on the quarterly report exceeds $2,500. Consequently, monthly deposits and tax forms must be processed through the bank and I. R. S.

2. The State Income Tax form is another factor. We'll use Ohio as an example. The state income tax on employees' wages must be reported on a quarterly basis. The form requires total employees' wages and sum of their tax deductions. Again, all forms must be filled out and sent (along with a check for the balance) and postmarked no later than January 31, April 30, July 31 and October 31. One has only about thirty days to complete the bookwork and mail the check. Be careful at this point. Some tax offices will require that all tax information and payments must be in their offices by the designated dates. The <u>date due</u> or <u>postmarked date</u> depends on the number of days in the month following the quarter.

The quarters are divided up into three months segment consisting of four reports. When the fourth quarter is reported, a summary for the year is required along with the final quarterly report. The first quarter constitutes January, February and March. It is due on April 30 of that same year. The second quarter runs from April through June. The taxes and payments for the second quarter are due on July 31. The third quarter's payments are due on (Oct. 31) which covers the months of July, August and September. The fourth quarter pertains to the year's final three months of October, November and December. The payment for them is due on the following January 31.

3. The next step is the city income tax form, which requests the gross wages forms, the city form requires uncompensated time from the employer, an envelope, and a postage stamp, also provided by the employer. The city also requires an annual summary.

One must be careful when filling out these forms and summaries as the federal, state and city forms may request information that could compromise a person's privacy. In doing so, the government is not in compliance with the Privacy Act passed in 1974. Therefore, the employer must be cautious not to include information regarding illegal activity, as well as correct any misdoings of federal, state and city employees concerning one's business personnel.

4. The form for Bureau of job and family services is due on a quarterly basis. This form requires employees' names, amount earned and number of weeks each employee worked. Any other information may intrude on an individual's privacy.

According to the aforementioned Privacy Act of 1974, it is illegal for the employer to volunteer information. The Social Security Administration advised that each individual must directly volunteer one's own Social Security number to agencies. The employer is only required to use it for Social Security purposes and not for identification as stated on the card issued.

However, the state collecting information illegally decided to ratify the federal law to fulfill their whiny ways. They had put the lives of all employers at stake. Every employer at the time before ratification who reported their employees' social security numbers to anyone but the Social Security department or the I.R.S. could probably have been sued for invasion of privacy.

The Bureau of job and family services said I was selected for an audit. Of course I thanked them for selecting me feeling I had something new to learn. However, when they came to audit, Campus Sundry was prepared. A form letter to be signed by the person obtaining information from our establishment that only our business could supply was presented.

It was out of complete necessity that this be put forward because of the Bushwhacked administration. Our freedoms and what America stands for are being eradicated while our constitution is being bastardized by idiots of no compassion, morals, ethics or integrity.

Our constitution has been in jeopardy for no reason other than to satisfy the whims of an out of touch, vindictive and lying administration. We must regain our lost allies. Again it is up to owners of small businesses in bringing this good earth back to the Promised Land that it once was.

The following was put forward:

Information on all our employees is kept confidential and all papers are given back to them when leaving. All information on our employees that are required by law are kept and then destroyed when the time limit is up. You will be responsible for anyone obtaining and seeing the data that is given under duress and what they do with it. Any invasion of privacy must not be tolerated.

Ethics: Campus Sundry considers employee confidentiality a top priority and ethics will be considered over law where necessary. We stand against release of any personal information for whatever reason other than the amount each individual makes and the amount of tax paid to a specific tax department. Any other information is only obtainable under ethical law.

Each employee of Campus Sundry will be given the name of auditor, department and a list of all information collected during an audit.

Campus Sundry wants the state employee to know that any information given during an audit is done under duress. Our applications assured all employees no personal information will ever be given to any department or individual for any reason. I as an employer will uphold their rights.

Once the examiner leaves the job for whichever he/she is representing, will be responsible for anyone who views the data of our employees that has been recorded. If it is damaging mentally or physically, the individual will have a right under Campus Sundry law and the personal privacy act of 1974 without its ratifications to do whatever is correct under the Ohio Revised Code and law provided all is ethical.

Campus Sundry will not be responsible for any information that is recorded under duress on its employees by any individual—whoever that may be. The department, in this case the Bureau of Job and Family services, will be responsible for any foul play when records are open to inspection by the director or the director's authorized representatives at any time.

Employer of this establishment realizes that in this global computer society that privacy becomes very important to each and every individual and will do whatever it takes to keep an employee's records private.

Person obtaining information in an audit _____
Department_____
Date and Time_____

5. A semi-annual report must be filled out and filed to the Workers Compensation Relief Fund. This pays for insurance if anyone is injured on the job. This form is unique because it requires employers to pay administrative costs along with the department's other costs. There are no personal questions asked on this form.

6. By February 1, the F. U. T. A. is due. This tax is due once a year. The F. U. T. A. stands for Federal Unemployment Tax Administration. The questions in filling out this form changes

almost yearly. Therefore the questions on the form must be read very carefully to successfully answer all the necessary information. However, in the recent years the questions have remained the same.

7. Each employer is required to keep a W-4 and I-9 form for each employee on file. These forms are filled out by the employee and returned to the employer. The number of exemptions each employee has is recorded on the W-4 form. The income tax chart is set up according to the number of employee exemptions. When calculating a payroll, the income tax chart is used to determine the amount of federal income tax to withhold. The bookkeeper goes across to the correct number of exemptions then traces down to the amount earned. This will give the amount to be withheld from the paycheck for federal income taxes.

At the end of the year, six W-2 forms are filled out per employee. These forms all have the total wages and taxes summed up on them. One form is for the federal government, one is for the employer and four are to go to the employee. It is then the employee's responsibility to file these forms in accordance with local, state and national laws. This considerable amount of bookwork is, of course, at the expense of the self-employed. The I-9 form is returned with proper identification proving that the employee is a legal citizen of the United States.

If the payroll is programmed into a computer, the amount earned is entered and it will present all tax deductions and net amount to be paid to an employee.

8. A summary of the four quarters determines the yearly report. This report includes total earnings and taxes deducted. It must be turned over to the local, state, and federal tax departments by January 31. One has just thirty-one days to answer forms and mail to each department respectively. Time and postage are just some of what is consumed by all of these tax laws.

9. The Personal Property Tax Form consists of the inventory at the end of the year. The form requests vast amounts of information to be filled out and filed by April 30. The tax has

to be paid by May 10. It can be paid in installments if one chooses to. Half is expected by May 10, while the other fifty percent is required by September.

10. Sales Tax Forms: In the state of Ohio, a 6.75% sales tax in Ohio is charged on all taxable sales. This has to be totaled at the end of each day, totaled monthly and sent to the tax office by the 23rd of each month that follows the month before. This means at least twelve mailings are required per year.

A brief explanation of this is as follows: Each employer adds the total sales tax taken in each month. A daily record is kept of this. It is simply a ledger with the amount of exempt sales, taxable sales, sales tax and the total sales. All four columns are then totaled at the end of the month. By the twenty-third of the following month, these totals are in the sales tax division of the department of taxation along with the check for the total sales tax. At the end of the year, an annual summary is reported.

Sales taxes are just another way for the tax departments to induce small business into doing free work for them. Menial tasks such as making the proper change to a customer may seem incidental when considered separately, but can become quite a nuisance in conjunction with all of the other burdens of a small business. Simple things like the amount of time it takes the clerk to figure out the proper amount of sales tax to be added can make a difference over time. All of these factors working in concert can take a financial, emotional and physical toll on a business practitioner. While the business owners are doing all the paperwork for the government, all the state has to do is enter the figures into a computer and deposit the tax check. Although sometimes the taxation division may incorrectly compute the report, the employer is responsible for the programmer's incompetence. In other words, the employer has to be accountable on both ends correcting all mistakes. If an employer's work is not done on time or if the check is not at the department of taxation by the twenty-third of the month, the merchant will be heavily penalized. There are very few exceptions and no exemptions.

Why Frustration Occurs:

We'll assume the sales tax department will notify one within twenty-three days if a mistake has occurred. It never quite works that way. According to a state worker, the sales tax department in the state of Ohio has forever to notify the taxpayer in the case of a discrepancy. This type of lackadaisical governing is annoying, and but all too common. Imagine the amount of interest and penalties that can and do accumulate. No government should have this amount of control over its people.

Getting any small business off the ground is very difficult. It requires much blood, sweat and tears. Perhaps even more taxing is the effort to keep one's business venture alive. There is not a day that goes by that does not present a serious challenge. This is why government intervention can be extremely frustrating. With the situation as tenuous as it is, emotions tend to run high. Many people in small business wonder why they must work so diligently for a government that has, at times, been so heavy-handed.

The state sales tax in Ohio amounts to 6.75% on taxable sales. The way the rates are set up, If an objective outside arbiter were to come into this situation, he/she would likely laugh at the quandary that we have been put in. We try to make enough money to survive without making so much that we are penalized. Unfortunately to those who live this life, the situation is anything but laughable. The bottom line is the countless hours spent making sales, doing bookwork, and filing forms are all costly and **thankless.**

Tax structure:

The tax structure is set the same way for small, medium-sized and big business. There was once a bill presented to Congress that would have paid employers $5 per form filed. Fearing fraud and corruption, Congress struck down the bill and the law never materialized. A law to pay employers for filling out forms would help to eliminate some of the financial burden to small businesses. Payments for forms filed by medium-sized or big business is probably financially obsolete.

The obligation of the entrepreneur of doing bookwork for the local, state and federal governments has increased steadily. All the forms that an employer is required to fill out have a deadline. Again, if a certain form is due or to be postmarked on a specific date, the bureaucracy will literally assess her/him for not being prompt.

A Certified Public Accountant may be hired to do this work. The cost depends on whatever the accountant wants to charge. Accountants are under the same obligations and restrictions as merchants. They are also self-employed. Even if a C.P.A. is hired, there is a certain amount of bookwork that has to be done before turning over to the accountant. Bookwork for the bureaucracy will always be a detriment to any self-employed person. The cost of doing the bookwork correctly for Uncle Sam will go on the liability side of the ledger.

One may now think that the bookwork is complete. Think again. If mistakes are made at any time, it is the employer's responsibility to clear the matter up. It is truly a case of guilty until proven innocent. This is why it is essential for any business owner to make extra sets of all tax returns. It is not unusual for a tax division to lose one's original form and ask for another copy. If this happens, the small-business owner is expected to sacrifice his/her time for a second time and spend one's money on postage. Also remember to send a copy of the canceled check (s) with the new form. If this does happen, it is important for the business owner to make the corrections in his/her personal records as well.

The government may go back four years on the FUTA tax. In 1990, I was asked about my 1986 returns. In '91, my '87 returns came into question. This same procedure lasted on and off through 1994. In every case, my records were absolutely accurate; yet, they persisted.

I was fortunate that my accounts were all in order. Others may not be as lucky. If the business return was in error, four years of accumulation of penalties and interest can lead a business straight into bankruptcy. This road of destruction is the only avenue the government has presented to small business. Compassion is never a consideration. In every instance, much time, energy and emotion was spent verifying what was known to be true.

A month is ample time to compute the tax forms. The government needs four years? If there is a mistake, the government owes any business person a chance for an explanation before any assessments are made. When one is doing the best possible work in the time allotted, it is an injustice for the government to impose an assessment of any kind.

Many years of business practice have taught me to file and pay my taxes on time. I have successfully done that on each occasion. However, there have been some snafus.

On October 10, 1988 the Internal Revenue Service wrongfully issued a notice of a lien for $1,500 dollars to my bank. The bank, in turn, withdrew the money from my business account by writing a check to the I.R.S. By the time they notified me of this action, the checks that I had written on the account were bouncing like basketballs, everywhere. This was not only personally mollifying, but financially disastrous as well.

On January 10, 1989, after three months of hardship and nasty communication back and forth, the I.R.S. phoned me. The lady informed me a mistake had been made and that they were "sorry for the inconvenience." That was all I got for enduring the frustration and embarrassment being accused of being a fraud.

"Sorry for the inconvenience" did not quite make up for not having enough money to afford a turkey for Thanksgiving or the gas to visit relatives at Christmas time. Between October 10, 1988 and the infamous January 10, 1989, my dispute with the I.R.S. became its nastiest. In that span I was called a liar, mentally abused, insulted and hung up on many times. Why should anyone be subjected to this type of treatment? The bottom line was that it was an I.R.S. error, not mine.

However, when it comes to taxes, it is very often the taxpayer's accountability to prove him or herself innocent more so than the prosecution's blame to prove one guilty. It was during that entire episode that I learned that the taxpayers' Bill of Rights is not worth the paper it is printed on. Any dealings with the I.R.S., even when you are right, will become a TRAUMATIC and horrific experience.

After the October 1988 incident, I began to lose touch with the customers and my employees. I was also having a tough time finding the hours necessary to accurately check inventory against sales. Those close told me that my feud with the Internal Revenue Service was ruining me emotionally. A silver lining in this dark cloud was that it allowed me to see how caring and helpful people close to me in my life are and how viciously vindictive arrogant perpetrators who lead unhappy lives can be. Although they were tired of listening to the whole ordeal, my friends remained faithful and patient throughout the whole mess. It was during this time that I decided to make this a political issue.

My Congressman was very supportive and gave me constructive feedback. Therefore it made no sense when people aired their horror stories involving the I.R.S. to the Senate Finance Committee for three days in 1997 on national television that the committee was oblivious to each and every situation.

To this day, there remains a bitter taste concerning the power someone may have over another individual. When the check was returned from the I.R.S., it said that it was for overpayment of taxes. It was returned for a notice of lien inaccurately issued on my account.

Years later I requested a copy of my records from the I.R.S. and noticed any evidence of the mistake had been shredded from the files. The lady's correspondence said there was no record of my business ever being assessed a lien. While my records remained in shambles as a result of the confrontation, the government's documentation of any such lien was non-existent. It was their position that this "lien" was little more than a figment of my imagination.

The notice of lien that was sent to the bank for payment had a signature on the line entitled *Chief Collection Agency* with the person's name. In time, I learned it was a fictitious person. This explained a lot of things about my battle with the Internal Revenue Service. Most notably, was that in the course of the entire fiasco I was never once connected with the person whose name appeared on the lien as the *Chief Collection Officer*.

This type of utter bureaucracy has made it nearly impossible for the businessperson to go without some kind of suffering if a blunder has occurred. This consternation happens regardless of which party is to blame. The entrepreneur has enough problems without government harassment. The result seems to be the taxpayer paying the government to be harassed. Small business should be celebrated for what it has done for the American economy over the years. Instead, it has been taken for granted and unnecessarily maligned and attacked in recent years. This type of governing is short sighted and ineffectual. It penalizes success to make everyone more "equal". It is destroying small business and the American economy with it.

In every discrepancy between the tax departments and the taxpayers, constructive communication on both sides is needed. Notifying the tax filer of a mistake immediately would enable him/her to reassess their findings and perhaps make a more accurate statement. It would go far in eliminating much of the financial strain and personal humiliation that have helped to cause the friction that currently exists between the nation's tax departments and its citizens.

With the technology that currently exists in America, this seems like an imminently plausible solution to this very serious problem. Such a solution would also likely reward those who file their returns early by giving them time to make the necessary adjustments. The most prominent reason for such a change is in the name of trust between the people and those that govern. It would only seem fair that one be permitted to correct an honest and minimal mistake without any sort of penalty and interest being tacked on.

A National Organization of Retailers could achieve success for the self-employed concerning the tax structure. The economic base that would be set up by N.O.R. would have to include a tax structure base. Questions on small matters could be addressed through a tax hotline. The self-employed wouldn't have to read a book just to fill out a form. With the elimination of such a huge burden entrepreneurs could focus their energies on other pressing needs of their respective businesses.

The National Organization of Retailers contingency would have one unique but crucial element. It would help its members, not simply govern them. Compassion and understanding would be some of the key components to its success. To state it simply, it would be a relationship between the organization and its members, not a business agreement. If such an organization were already in place, there is no telling where small enterprise would be today. Then again, if such a logical solution had already been implemented, there would be little need for this book. As things are, there are some solutions out there that can make a real difference in our business and in our lives.

The poet Clement Clark Moore, author of many renowned works, (perhaps most notably *'Twas the Night before Christmas*), once wrote that "destiny was a matter of choice, not chance." That is where small business is as an entity. The bureaucrats in Washington do not control the destiny of small business. **Small business controls the destiny of**

small business. For too long, that has meant we have allowed ourselves to be fragmented and disorganized. And for too long we have been continuously targeted for our stubbornness as a result. The National Organization of Retailers affords us the opportunity to change this. It is now our turn to summon up the courage and resolve to capitalize on this opportunity.

The cliché 'life is not fair' will be reinstated to 'life is fair.".. Where there is power and money, there's corruption. The inability to ostracize this obstacle has left many in an enigma. I sincerely believe that owners of small business can make an impact on the economy landscape by not letting greed interfere with capitalism and its reward.

Vital Importance:

It would seem that the tax laws of this country change almost daily. For this reason, it is paramount that one always read all of the writing on every form that one lends a signature to. It is also essential that one meet all the deadlines established by the tax forms. Remember when filing some will read, **"Must be post marked before said date"**, while others will say **"Due in the tax office on or before date given"**. These deadlines are serious and inflexible. If one fails to meet the issued deadline, one can rest assured that they will be assessed a penalty.

Summary of tax forms:
   Federal:
1. An Employer Tax Identification Number is issued when the employer registration forms are filled out.
2. I-9 form (Employment Eligibility Verification)—Form is issued by the immigration office to be filled out by the employee and kept on file by the employer. Form is used to ensure that the employee is a legal U. S. citizen. A fine of $100 is billed to the employer for each I-9 form not on file.
3. W-4 form—The form is to be prepared by the employee and kept on file by the employer. It is used to indicate the number of exemptions for the employee and to determine the tax to be withheld.
4. The employer prepares W-2 forms. There are six forms on each individual, prepared annually: one form for the Internal

Revenue Service; b. one form for the employer; and c. four forms for the employee.

5. W-3 form is prepared annually and is a summary of all the W-2 forms.

6. Form 941—Federal Quarterly Payroll Taxes. All wages and taxes on employees' pay are reported quarterly to the Internal Revenue Service: (a) First quarter—January, February, March—due, filed and paid on or before April 30. (b) Second quarter—April, May, June—due, filed and paid on or before July 31. (c) Third quarter—July, August, September—due, filed and paid on or before October 31. (d) Fourth quarter—October, November, December—due, filed and paid on or before January 31.

Monthly tax deposits must be made if the quarterly tax balance due is over $2,500; thus, a form and a check must be prepared on a monthly basis and mailed to the I.R.S. If the quarterly report balance is still over $2,500 dollars, an assessment has occurred. The I.R.S. will notify the employer.

7. A federal form must be completed for the year. This has to be filed and returned with W-2 forms by January 31, to the Social Security administration. Form requires every employee's name, Social Security number, wages, deductions and net pay.

8. FUTA—Federal Unemployment Tax Administration is one form that must be filed and paid on or before January 31.

9. All forms for the April 15 tax return (income of the prior year) also included with the 1040 form are a profit and loss statement for the business. You can file form 4868, which permits a six-month extension for filing. However, all money due must be mailed with the extension form postmarked on or before April 15th.

State:

1. A quarterly report for state taxes deducted from each employee's paycheck is due the same as federal tax returns. Check to see if by the date on the form is says postmarked or due.

2. End of the year summary forms for the state are also due. There is more than one.

3. The Bureau of Employment Services' form is due quarterly, and is the same as federal. This form's due date reads must be postmarked.
4. State sales tax must be reported monthly and filed and paid by the 23rd day of the following month. This means it is due 12 times a year. No extensions are granted in the state of Ohio. There are heavy fines for any delays, with no recourse.
5. The Bureau of Workers' Compensation form and money is due semi-annually (or twice a year). Again date must be checked as to when it needs to be postmarked or if it reads due. The employer pays workers' compensation administration costs. Total of six months payroll multiplied by percentage set up by the BWC is the amount due each half year.
6. Commercial Activity Tax: Each business grossing less than $1 million in sales each year is liable for $150 surtax, while those grossing over $1 million must pay a percentage of their gross sales. It replaces a 0.5% sales tax reduction, which of course is great for consumers who do not pay this activity tax. Therefore, the financial burden is *quietly* put on the business owners.

Local:
1. These quarterly tax forms are the same as the federal and state.
2. A summary form at the end of each year is due on or before January 31, the following year.
3. Personal Property Tax forms are due April 30. This is an inventory of stock for the beginning of the year. Half of the taxes are due May 10, and half are due by September.

Other forms and taxes:
1. Vendor's License
2. Vendor's License yearly renewal
3. Permits that are needed would depend on the type of business. Examples are: cigarette license, Hotel and Motel licenses, food licenses, health permits, alcohol permits, rental permits, carry-out license, gambling permits or licenses and university licensed sportswear.

None of these taxes for licenses and permits required of the business people are a profit in themselves. They are financial detriments consuming money, valuable time, work and energy. These taxes pay for a federal, state or local department that, in itself, is unnecessary.

An understanding of all the tax laws is essential. All taxes, if not filed and paid on time, carry huge assessments. Congress bestows on the self-employed tax revisions from time to time. The newest developments in tax laws change daily.

Congress needs to be reshaped and regrouped to inspirer leaders of small business. We need supportive politicians. We need a Congress that represents all sectors of the economy. Entrepreneurs need leaders with compassion and appreciation for all of the work business people do for the government. If the owners of small business grouped together as entrepreneurs of business enterprise, National Organization of Retailers, the impact of lobbyists in Washington would carry more influence than all the other associations combined.

If one can afford a CPA, it would be advisable. It is foolish for small businesses to even pay state taxes. It seems like all of the money that we are paying is serving to further subjugate ourselves. Much of the taxes we pay are then allocated to state universities who are in turn making forays into small business. In essence, educational institutions have evolved into corporations (business workshops) in direct competition with small business. The unfortunate but brutal irony of this is that this would seem to be terribly unethical for institutions whose core responsibility to its constituents is teaching them ethics. There is a positive side to all of this. A university operated small business venture would likely be forced into sizable taxes at some point in time. It is our hope that the government would use this opportunity to help out other worthy organizations (i.e. N.O.R.). This sort of unprecedented role reversal would help small business to create many of the benefits and amenities that are so long overdue to employers and employees of small shops. Obviously, any member of such an establishment university owned would not be eligible to join the N.O.R. The employees of such an institution would come under the heading of 'Industrial workshops' run by a big conglomerate unrelated in any way to owners of small enterprises.

Ethics is a blessed virtue. Repetition of this issue to clear many points will occur in other parts of this book. Both the American Dream and ethics have become distorted; therefore, in many cases the word <u>real</u> as an adjective must proceed. It's displeasing but for restoration purposes it's feasible.

Webster describes ethics as "(1) a body of moral principles or values (2) a moral precept or rule of conduct." The dictionary denotes moral to mean "(1) of or concern with the principles of right and wrong conduct (2) conforming to principles of right conduct (3) capable of recognizing and conforming to the rules of right conduct." In the N.O.R. real ethics by a code of conduct will rule or be the guide. Any continuance of unethical behavior or misrepresentation of an association's leaders will not be tolerated and dismissal is evident.

A national sales tax would put an end to the fiasco government entities have established. Assuming it replaces all other taxes on a permanent status would be favorable to small businesses throughout the country.

Once you establish a business and add employees the tax departments start you on a treadmill that keeps going faster and faster without intervals. Small businesses' deepest nightmare is taking on the responsibility of all issues timely filed and paid on their employees.

Edmond Burke said, "The greater the power, the more dangerous the abuse." Inefficiency and harassment in the tax system is overwhelming to the point where tolerance is not a good scenario. If we unite and stay together we survive.

Tax departments are very stern and arrogant. There are a few tax consultants that seem to take an interest in the tax payer's dilemma. However, humor is nonexistent.

CHAPTER 6

INTRODUCTION
UNIFICATION

Retailers uniting are as American as baseball,
hot dogs, apple pie, marijuana and beer.

The self employed would greatly benefit by establishing a National Organization of Retailers An association would allow us to participate in our own destination. Applying the golden rule, "Do unto others as you would have others do unto you" oust any irrational treatment.

United we stand, divided we fall

Due to the fact that this bureaucracy is seizing every penny from hard working individuals leaves no doubt that other professions are feeling the bite. Even badly needed doctors and lawyers are performing double duty leaving no pause for relaxation and family.

The cost of living is forever on the rise. Government employees enjoy generous wage increases while the self-employed paychecks are diminishing. A pay freeze in 2011 has been put in place, but a pay reduction is also in order. Employers work over one hundred hours a week just to put food on the table. This is hardly the American way. Smaller paychecks and longer hours have become an American nightmare not a dream. Uniting is the solution.

Remedy + Repetition = Reward

Politicians, Health departments and other entities that advocate sending in a seventeen year old person to buy cigarettes from a retailer are asking for trouble. Unethical treatment such as putting a person's security at risk by entrapment is ludicrous and bizarre. Vindictive legislators dominating small business, yet supporting large affluent corporations, have retailers in the lurch;

Retailers in the lurch have no defense

Once we get an association, we will join all the other associations. If necessary, our numbers will be the majority: thus we can vote for leaders that support the American Dream. It may not be a Democrat or Republican, but America is desperate for leaders that walk the talk without side stepping.

PART I

Small business once served as a comfortable and willing cornerstone upon which America rested. The changing economic and social structures America underwent in recent years have ended that romantic time in our history. The comfortable old deli, a place locals would socialize and mingle, has now given way to super-convenience or mega-stores. People no longer want to be bothered with socializing. Instead, many prefer to purchase and leave. This has permeated throughout every level of society.

With trust between citizens having gone the way of the dinosaurs, many organizations have been forced to unify for protection. The result has predictably been a rise in the social and political status of those organizations. For professions that have elected to remain independent of each other, their status has remained unaltered. In the case of small business, our status has actually slipped as a result of this cultural shift.

Besides relieving many of the burdens a profession faces, organizations also help to alleviate many of the pressures and time constraints a business person encounters. If small business were to unify into such an organization, independent entrepreneurs would be free to focus their energies on more pressing and beneficial issues.

The small business landscape is proving it needs assistance, and that means individuals grouping together for the longevity. Leadership, integrity, ethics and progressive planning would all come into play to create a better environment in which to work.

The services that an association can offer have been earned by doctors, lawyers, teachers, auto workers, nurses, plumbers, electricians, engineers and others over the years. Their successful unity is due, in large part, to the fact that their associations were built slowly with strong foundations. All of these organizations have had the advantage of energetic, dedicated and loyal leadership.

An association could serve as the principal reason for success in one's given field. Small businesses are falling by the wayside in droves. The industry is proving it needs a well thought out plan to progressively move forward.

A well organized association can help to curb and hopefully put an end to this mounting problem. Uniting does not mean that the N.O.R. can end the death of small business; thus, it means that the odds of success for owners of small business are much greater if supported by a powerful organization.

The association would provide assistance with each individual's problems with other entities such as tax departments and legal aid where needed. If this now essential association had organized years ago, there is no telling how many higher levels of success owners of small businesses would have enjoyed.

Many businesses that are now in danger of folding could prosper under this new system. Success that now so easily eludes entrepreneurial could suddenly become very attainable.

A National Association of Retailers would be a stronger backbone for the economy, providing security for every self-employed person in the United States. Millions of shop owners belonging to an organization that operates on a constructive and progressive basis would offer a sense of protection for each member.

The most vital resource the association will provide in its base structure is information on all business problems. This diverse structure will permit freedom for constituents who seek it and guidance for those who clamor for it. Amenities like eight hundred numbers, web sites and E-mail will be set up to help with questions and provide for answers and information one might seek.

N.O.R. business officials will have a very strong will and provide hands-on experience. This can include anything from responding to a few telephone calls to handling more complex problems. Millions of entrepreneurs belonging to an organized group that operates constructively would project a sense of security.

Answers will be given in a timely manner on all issues at the local, regional and federal levels. Authorities of the association would be available 24/7, not just during a limited time period. Answering machines, voice mail and the likes, would be far too impersonal for this systemization. The services and benefits to its members would be as easily available. Legal, accounting, banking and insurance agencies would all be developed within the affiliation. The structure would also provide a service element that would offer services in person (if needed) to support the business person in one's given endeavor.

Research into the day-to-day operation of other national alliances would be recommended so that proven ideas can be used along with the creation of new ones. The result would hopefully be aggressive, fresh, practical and well organized with the aim of helping small business. Whatever the discrepancy, an association is a positive way to resolve it.

Entrepreneurs deserve to come together and to stop fighting amongst themselves. A flexible national group would be a huge benefit to all businesses. A cohesive business community makes for a healthy economy that in turn would help everyone involved. As things stand now, our independent purchasing of products would be cheapened substantially if we bought in bulk, or wholesalers provided better incentives. Instead, we are paying inflated flat rates as a result of little purchasing power.

We often hear about members of Congress and their discussion and consultation with the medical community. The same is true about the legal and teaching community. When these organizations talk, the government listens. Why does one suppose that is? Is it because the government has great reverence for those positions and would like to appease them? Maybe, but my far more cynical side suggests that these are politicians seeking political allies. The American Medical Association, the American Bar Association and the National Education Association provide a nice pillar of support for any catering politician.

With the sheer number of retailers in the country, it is almost absurd that we have been ignored. Yet, the record speaks for itself. When legislation is passed for a particular sector of the economy, it is always a reaction to pressure from some organization. Retailers need to find a way to take the unique attributes of diversity and independence and unite them to work for us, not against us. If we are successful in accomplishing this, we will be a gigantic powerhouse.

As mentioned in previous chapters, many other professions have national representation in Washington, D. C. The small business sector is not amongst that contingent. An owner of small business acts alone in everything he or she does. In another day, the independence served as an attractive advantage of owning one's own business. That era is over, however, and many small businesses are unable to weather this economic storm without the umbrella of a unified group to protect them.

Stores that informed the Security Exchange of closings October 2008 to January 2009 have no relief from the government. Congress is only interested in bailing out the corrupt billionaires. Politicians say one thing to get elected, but once in office hardly ever fulfill their promises.

Lobbyists are needed in Washington D.C. to make an impact on the capital's legislators. The first step in that direction is with good marketing research. Merchants first need to send field agents out to research what the latest trends are in small business. This report must also include recommendations as to what can be done to improve our situation. Such a study is necessary to the life of small business in America.

Each small retail store is accountable to the same number of tax forms as larger enterprises. The process is much more costly to self-employed independently owned businesses than it is to the larger corporations.

Retailers need an organization that includes a tax base. Groups that can challenge alliances like the I.R.S. in case an employer makes a mistake. The expanding tax laws remain the merchant's principal objection. Congressional attempts to tax small businesses has at the very least, indirectly caused many small businesses to falter.

A small business agency could ensure that every employer has an ultimatum and is given ample time to correct any discrepancy prior to action being taken against them and rightfully so. Now, if an error is made, the retailer has to pay a penalty and interest called an assessment. The agency's job would be to protect its members' right to justify and correct any mistake before an assessment is carried out.

Communication is ineffectual and wasteful if it does not allow for change. Most people have far more to offer the world than they realize. An organization with leaders willing to accept input from its members is meaningful for changes.

Capitalism is the best economic plan in the world, but it is far from perfect. Our forefather's economic ideas were both honorable and noble. Their system was unique and designed to reward the merits of laborious and dedicated individuals. However, our congressional government today has small business surfing on sand. You got it. No way. If small business doesn't build an association by bringing the largest group of people together, there is probably no other hope for success unless it is divine intervention.

As the country has grown and changed, small business has seen its financial rewards decreasing. Pressure has been put on the middle. That middle happens to be right where the small business lies. Programs intended to help some of the members of the lower sector of the economy were well intended but grossly mismanaged.

An establishment that can restore faith, compassion, virtue and humanity to the nation's middle class is sadly needed. The American Dream is more than a matter of finance. It is an ideal way of life. The dream is about happiness, not just contentment. It is about positive believing as well as positive thinking. Most of all, the American Dream is about togetherness, ethics and understanding that once was and still can be the social fabric of our society.

Any person who undertakes a commercial risk for profit knows the course of events that occur when a tax department goes beyond the law. No one is above the law; however, no one is below the law. Maliciousness is the tax department and most of their employee's way of life. The nature of retail is that it forces one to take quick and decisive steps toward solving problems. With constant pressure from the job as well as the government, owners of small business have all been well trained in the importance of punctuality. We are a society that, like journalism, faces constant deadlines. Now we face another deadline—that of empowerment. <u>Our opportunity is upon us and it is time to act. As is so often the case, this opportunity will not last forever, and there will be no extensions.</u>

Where did our hard earned tax money go? We all know the answer. It was given to the rich that are unfit to hold the CEO, CFO and executive offices who bankrupted their companies. None were charged for misdoings, but rewarded for their incompetence. Regardless no business can let expenses exceed profits

In 2010 and the past few years the business community needs help. This could be misleading because help in the way of loans for entrepreneurs is unwise during a recession/depression. Stores have ample inventory and don't need another debt, nor mega store competition but more customers that spend.

A misconception of the need for success has evaded the call for help. To take on another debt would be disastrous. Time has come to put people back to work. America needs jobs. Tarp eliminated millions of jobs for the poor; bankrupt the economy, seizing smaller banks where millions lost jobs while misguiding our tax money from the poor to the rich (Robin Hood in reverse) making the rich richer and a deeper depression for the poor

People would support their American small stores by purchasing goods instead of wishful thinking window shopping provided they have jobs. Pressures like never before have stifled the shops across the country because the peoples' buying power are limited. There are no jobs to produce money.

2010 and 2011 did not see a cost of living increase in Social Security paychecks. However, legislators picking on older people gave themselves a raise. Again the tax money is wasted.

Our forefathers laid the ground work only to have it destroyed by AIG, banks, auto industries, bailouts and nothing for the struggling hard working people

Arrogance is not the protocol. No trails have been put forward. No one has been prosecuted. The defense rests for lack of work. Somewhere in America there must be salvation. Many over-paid individuals should be punished not rewarded for bankrupting the company's financial resources.

More will be discussed about mismanagement being rewarded in Chapter 24. Many are interested in where tax money is going. Pumping into the rich while the poor literally have no food. America needs new leaders unlike the present and past administrations; thus excluding the great President Bill Clinton and his magnificent staff who eliminated our debt and deficit leaving a substantial amount of money when he left office.

PART II

NATIONAL ORGANIZATION OF RETAILERS

*"The more one considers such an organization,
the less sense it makes not to have had one."*

Broadcast Journalist James T. Cromie

"Coming together is a beginning.
Keeping together is progress.
Working together is success."

Henry Ford

"None of us is as smart as all of us"

Anonymous or Unknown

"A hundred times a day I remind myself that my life depends on the labors of other people, and that I must exert myself to give, just as I have received."

Albert Einstein

"We didn't all come over in the same ship,
but here we are in the same boat."

Anonymous or Unknown

"Build with your team a feeling for oneness, of dependence on one another, and strength from unity in the pursuit of your objectives."

Football Coach Vince Lombardi

"I skate to where the puck is going to be, not where it has been."

Hockey great Wayne Gretzky

PART II

Small business has served as a sort of prodigal son of "Uncle Sam." We have been treated accordingly. Though it may be hard to believe, it is not the government's fault. People are treated the way they permit. The fault clearly lies with small business. Our inability to organize has made us economically and politically impotent. The government does not have a vendetta against small business; it is simply capitalizing on the existing structure.

The government is either ignorant to, or callous of, their handling of small business. In 1997 new legislation was passed regarding cigarettes that affected millions of retailers throughout the nation. The law calls for any person selling cigarettes to a patron who appears to be 26 or younger to check the identification of the purchaser. Of course, if the buyer is under eighteen, store owners are prohibited from selling them cigarettes. To enforce these new regulations some police and health departments gather groups of minors to pose as adults and are instructed to attempt to buy cigarettes. This is not only entrapment, it isn't fair to the kids involved. Any business owner who feels that the livelihood of one's business is threatened over a cigarette sale is not likely to be happy. When provoked, people can be vicious. It would be tragic if one of these young men or women was hurt by an irate and desperate shop owner.

Fines of $250 dollars and suspensions of buy back contracts by manufacturers present an expense very few honorable merchants can afford. We are not talking about owners who cater to underage people buying cigarettes for the success of their business.

The psychology of this new legislation is neither sophisticated nor reverse. The impact is paranoia. Now all customers are first looked upon by the clerk as an entrapment device until carded and proven innocent. This wastes time and energy that is needed elsewhere. Foresight is an ever important issue when new legislation is supported. The paranoia is self-preservation.

The money could be better spent by helping the clerks with checking individuals who are underage. Assistance in a constructive method is beyond the people who are against the establishment. Who needs it?

No employee has the capabilities of working to his or her potential in a tense environment. The chain of the work force is further weakened. It is hard to comprehend why our tax money is used for harassment. Working against instead of for an establishment is in no way constructive.

With all of these sanctions and regulations in full operation, there is not even remotely conclusive evidence that supports that this practice has curbed the underage smoking problem in American. In fact, fifteen months later, youth smoking had increased considerably according to reports. In short, there is another bureaucratic hoop to jump through that is ineffective and fruitless while being detrimental to retailers.

The American government is so big that it sometimes fails to realize the full effect of its legislation. Sir Isaac Newton's third law of motion is written in its alternative translation: "Every action has an equal and opposite reaction."

Newton obviously never dealt with the legislation of our government. Entrepreneurs are suffering from an unmanageable information overload. The overload occurs when legislation comes from the right, the left and then through the middle. Shop owners are unable restrain the force of the legislation. Thus, the reaction to the legislation generates nil resistance, leaving the action in perpetual motion. We manage to complete our lessons through perseverance.

This is the story of how business and government have interacted over the years. In an effort to fix their previous bureaucratic blunders, Congress continually passes more legislation that only helps to compound the existing problems. Many feel that as time has passed, Congress is not only unable to fix problems; they have come to personify them.

Reversing the present process of retailers' infinite regression involves focusing on a new unified procedure. After all, small business is nowhere on the scale of political priorities. The time has come to throw business legislation at government legislation and reinstate Newton's theory of motion.

It should be clear by now that the best possible route for small business to take is toward organization. Until that happens, all of the subsidies and incentives issues will continue to benefit other professions. These are professions that organized themselves long ago. It is not a coincidence that the better organized an association is, the more breaks seem to go their way.

With concrete base structures, the business foundation will have a balanced life of honesty and integrity we never before have enjoyed. The result promises to be a more competent, confident and potent life for shops throughout the nation. Without an association, we will continue to meander along with the same obstacles plaguing us in the future that have always slowed us down in the past with new hurdles to overcome. Imminently solvable problems have grown into insurmountable road blocks for no reason other than our unwillingness to unite as one heterogeneous mass.

In its present state, government appears to be anti-small business and favors corporate greed. Supporting huge political campaign funds for candidates by big business has become the American way of life. The revivification of trust can develop through a National Organization of Retailers.

Collective bargaining does work for Labor relations. The United Parcel Service's fifteen day strike in August, 1997 was settled by workers standing together. Small-business owners have no negotiators. Although the U. P. S. strike could have been prevented through better communications between labor and management, members were spellbound by corporate greed.

This type of malice by the anti-small business sector has enchanted the entrepreneur work force for decades. Retailers remain silenced because they have no means of securing constructive arbitration. The government does not have the ability to rescue the long forgotten American Dream of combining business prosperity with family harmony; therefore, proprietorship economics will be top priority after unification of a N. O. R. With the elimination of greed, communications will be meaningful.

In my many years of experience I have not seen a single law that has been passed in favor of small business. In the interim, law after law has been passed to help other professions. While most Americans' working days have decreased, many entrepreneurs working hours have increased along and with a pay lower than minimum wage. Legislation has made other professions far less difficult and more financially rewarding. Conversely, the average small-business owner's work load is enough to drive any sane person mad. The many hours required to properly bureaucratize is absurd, and costs the owners of small businesses money, energy and restless sleep.

Growth, along with change, may be a key concept of this entire book. As the bureaucracy and the bookkeeping grow, the health of business and the economy cannot. The minimization of these peripheral concerns is the key to the blossoming of American business. A unified group with a voice in Washington D.C. may be the only way to ensure that this happens. An organization that is functional and progressive is the best path the traditionally conservative retailers can take. Such an entity would have to be fraught with people of honesty, compassion, understanding and integrity to succeed permitting ethics to reign supreme. Fortunately, small business seems to attract just that type of unflappable personality. A small business association that is run properly could be a business saver for many who choose to join it.

The leaders of this National Organization of Retailers would have to be selfless and tireless in preserving a togetherness that small-business owners have never before experienced or enjoyed.

The protection and preservation of a solid foundation to stabilize the entrepreneur is essential. Base structures are obviously the major prerequisites of building this association. For this reason, the growth must be slow and steady in the early stages to ensure more rapid growth as the alliance matures.

If such a support system were already available, many businesses that have fallen by the way side over the years may have been able to use the organization as a crutch in trying times. Needed support was never available. Some businesses are so frail they cannot make any mistakes in the initial stages. Errors can be costly. An unified group of small business practitioners may help alleviate that problem by offering their colleague sound advice as to what steps one can take to land on one's feet financially. Consequently, many failed ventures of the past may still be in operation and thriving today with the N.O.R.'s help.

Yesterday is over while tomorrow relentlessly pursues us. A small business cannot continue to clamor for days past. Perhaps this is "Father Times" cruelest lesson. Lord Bryon warned us, "Nostalgia is a seductive liar". Nowhere is this more evident than in our society. As citizens of the new millennium America seem to have far more problems than it does solutions, we are constantly reminded of a time that never truly was, but should have been. If Remedy + Repetition = Reward had been in play, then many problems would have never occurred.

The humor of the whole situation is when political leaders continuously repeat over, over and over the same problems for decades. If they spent as much energy on a remedy, the solutions would overtake the problems. How long have we been hearing Social Security is in trouble? Saving Social Security is as elementary as ABC.

If government keeps their hands out of the pot, ample funds would be available to the recipients as President Roosevelt designated. Congress should display some strength in Social Security.

The transformation from the forward looking fifties to the introspective sixties to the confused and self-absorbed seventies and eighties trying to keep up with the hurling technological advances in the nineties have led America to its current stage of helpless independence and yearning in this new millennium.

We live in an era where people are willing to go on national television to air their dirty laundry. A senator was on a television talk show airing his dirty laundry to promote a book he wrote. The accuracy of the conversation was questionable. After thirty-plus years he should have put it to rest. The method to this apparent madness is to show we can never go back.

Old solutions do not always solve new problems. Instead of wasting time wistfully discussing how things used to be, we should focus on how life can be. This is not to denigrate our past in any way. It is simply meant to illustrate times have changed and so has our society. Old staples like the neighborhood store and the front porch have given way to quickie-marts and something called a "stoop". Our "Microwave Society" has become obsessed with convenience at the expense of interpersonal relationships. Small businesses must recognize this social shift of people wanting to buy and leave, or prepare for a loss of business.

Shops continue to sprout up like branches on a gigantic economic tree. The livelihood of each is at least indirectly intertwined with the health of the others. An organization would allow these many separate branches to unite cohesively, allowing the entire tree to take root and blossom. In time, this continuous growth may lead into an entire forest of healthy trees. Without this necessary growth, small businesses will continue to feel like they are out on a limb.

Congress could have created an advisory board for small business, but does not understand the intricacies of running a store even though some politicians have relatives who own small businesses. Although these sons and daughters are leaders of the nation, they seem unable to help their relatives especially the mothers and fathers who raised them.

These sons and daughters talk about their parents to further their own careers. That's the extent of their family assistance. Their focus is distorted. If they can't help their own, then there is no way they can assist any honorable entrepreneurial.

The obstacles that loom so large should have never existed. An association such as the N.O.R. has the potential to make the proprietor's American Dream a reality.

American entrepreneurs are like pieces of a puzzle scattered all over America. The puzzle remains in pieces. The governmental bureaucracy serves as a locked box that stifles and smothers these pieces. We must open this box and piece this puzzle together before we can begin to move forward into a better and more certain tomorrow.

Small business owners will have no peace until all the pieces of the puzzle are put together. The neoclassic puzzle transforming into a bright, gigantic, picturesque mosaic would even astonish and delight the famous painter/sculptor Michelangelo.

A well organized business association with mentally coherent and open management is tantamount to the stabilization and expansion of our idea. Communications between all of the organization's members and dedication to the group's cause will allow this movement to succeed.

The earth is God's garden. It must be tended to, nourished and protected with ethics, honesty and integrity. These elements are missing in today's society. An entrepreneur is a segment of that garden capable of providing such a trust. The nourishment can be channeled though constructive guidance, protection and direction for retailers.

A National Organization of Retailers with the entrepreneurs as its leaders would have the necessary ingredients and ample experience to focus in on many of the problems at present.

The leaders at N.O.R. will not be millionaires, nor will they be treated as such. We will leave those types of personalities for the "Fortune 500" companies. Our leaders will be paid well, but not excessively. The lifestyles of our leaders will mirror the hard work and dedication that any independent business owner exerts every day.

Freebies will not be part of the N.O.R. leadership role. Things like travel expenses and free business dinners will simply not be a part of the National Association for Retailers. This organization is not to be built to appease the "fat cat" leaders.

The N.O.R. hierarchy will reflect the integrity and dedication of its constituents. Many will believe that the N.O.R. stands for the National Organization of Retailers, but it really will stand for family.

Family plays a larger role in the American culture than small business. Just as many small businesses that are scattered throughout this land collectively serve as America's economic background; it is the nuclear family unit that serves as this nation's social background. Without strength in both it would be hard for small business to survive.

Dinners are places where a family can really get to know each other: It has been said that our strongest bonds are tied as we eat. Eating dinner with someone is an intimate experience and should be viewed as one. Therefore, it is inexcusable when a business person elects to dine with a client rather than his or her own flesh and blood. Today, the essence of family values is used loosely.

Business people will fly commercial. No private jumbo jets, no raises bonuses or perks only when the organization is showing profit that is substantial. Business people have given up something along the way to get to where they want to be. Entrepreneurs are unlike big corporations giving under achievers raises, bonuses and perqs. regardless of company's profit or loss. Owners of small business all to often have to take a lesser paycheck than the year before.

If entrepreneurs gave themselves raises with bonuses every year, then a shop losing money is highly unlikely to survive. The pay has to be adjusted to the yearly profit or loss. It's mysterious as to how executives that fail are heavily rewarded.

Small business does not have the luxury of a bailout from the federal government; therefore, an entrepreneurial organization could support shops in time of need. Bailout was two words until government interfered.

An unhealthy business or deficit operation is one sure way to achieve disaster. Does big business understand? I think not. The culprits take their big paychecks, bonuses and millions of dollars worth of perquisites regardless of the status of the company. And why shouldn't they? They will be retired with their many homes and millions when the corporation faces bankruptcy. No sweat here. Our stupid and greedy administration will bail them out.

Cannot understand why leaders in corporations and universities receive high paychecks, perqs. (perquisites) and bonuses as the organizations are losing money because of the culprits' mismanagement.

The hypothesis bailout Wall Street it will trickle down to Main Street is a myth. Executives have a field day with the money. More raises, bonuses and perks for the rich at the expense of the poor. Congress needs to allocate where the money is spent. Past experience of the dilemma requires proper research as to where the money was wrongly spent from the ground up. Congress doesn't have the experience as most are lawyers with very little knowledge in business.

The N.O.R. will adhere to the golden rule. In N.O.R.'s formative years, each person that owns a small business will donate no less than $100 annually, but no more than $200. Dues will be added to help further enhance this group of players. The group formed whenever a network is established. Services for law, medicine and banking will be picked up by the organization. This system could replace the quite expensive, independent professionals currently employed by small businesses. This system would produce great savings in time, money, patience and stress.

Proposing another cost is hard on small-business owners. However, the small financial investment will measure up to the largest profit encountered by its contributors. In the long term of financial savings the everlasting security goal will bond N.O.R. with stability, respect and most importantly, a voice not to be taken lightly. Like the N.E.A., A.B.A. and A.M.A. the N.O.R. fabric will be permanently interwoven.

For the financial structure to work, the costs of the services in the base structure of a self-employed organization cannot and will not exceed the dues. The costs for everything will be paid for by the association from the organization's membership dues. National appointees will constitute the governing body of N.O.R. There will also be positions designated at the state, local and sectional levels. If the organization cannot operate within the budget, it will not survive.

Once a small business burgeons into a big business, N.O.R. will no longer consider it a member. There is nothing wrong with capitalizing on a highly successful operation. N.O.R. simply cannot offer its umbrella of support and protection to a company that does not truly need it.

Although entrepreneurships of all ages are on the rise, an organization would generate new radiant light for success. Risk would be lower. To better improve their communities, entrepreneurs could volunteer giving time back. Small businesses need help. Assistance would revolutionize and energize the business landscape. America would again become the land of great opportunity.

Quoting broadcast journalist James T. Cromie, "The more one considers such an organization, the less sense it makes not to have had one". An objective point of view tells the whole story.

PART III

Let's talk the talk, and walk the walk

PART III

Walk the walk
Let's not side step the talk

Globalization: We've not only had our privacy invaded, our security threatened, jobs going overseas, smoking privileges confined and untruths told to us, while foreign imports are destroying our own economy. The American Dream has become an incredible and sometimes unreachable challenge.

Many have lost their jobs. Job loss is one of the main reasons that most people want to go into independent business.

Self-destruction is boiling over as imports are becoming the center of shopping—American's Favorite Pastime. Goods from other countries have usurped American made items by selling at a lower price. Take a reality check. Check the labels on your purchases and you'll find that most of the merchandise say, "Made in China," "Made in India" or made elsewhere other than the United States. It is only a matter of time before many cars that we purchase will be made in China or India at a lesser expense to the American people than Japan's Toyota, Honda and Nissan. The auto makers in the American sector "per se" may be in deeper jeopardy.

While we are helping China, Japan, India and other foreign countries increase their economies, we are doing this at the expense of our own United States economy. More and more businesses are closing because of Mega Stores with their inventory of imported stock.

As an owner of a small business, it appears that government favors mega-stores over small business; thus, allowing big businesses many options that small businesses have been deprived or cannot afford. Yet, many of us already in business have not made a move to build an association and stop the 'fat cats' from locking the doors of entrepreneurial dreams.

Owners of small business must unite before the long awaited dream is lost forever. While more and more people are talking about jobs going overseas they are neglecting the real reason jobs are being lost. The low cost of merchandised imports has American business in a downward spiral. American manufacturers cannot compete. The high costs of labor and goods have kept them out of competition with the inexpensive foreign products; therefore, many manufactures have to relocate in other countries in order to prosper.

Purchases from American manufacturing cannot keep escalating across the board forever. We have priced ourselves out of higher education, homes, cars, luxuries, necessities and families 24/7 quality time not because of capitalism, but greed. Guidelines set up by a lackadaisical, uncaring and overpaid Congress favoring (the pay is nothing, compared to the large amount of perquisites and bonuses) mega-stores have small business in a lurch.

It is only a matter of time before all manufacturing jobs will relocate in an area overseas and manufacturing in America will be gone. When it happens then our overseas suppliers will be able to charge any amount they want when selling to the United States. Is anyone listening?

Yes, a National Organization of Retailers is long overdue. One of its main functions is security. Putting our wide range of personalities together, we become strong politically, economically and socially.

Risks are a large part of our industry. Many of us have overcome the obstacles that stand in our way as individual proprietors; thus, it is time to unite, put our noses to the grindstone and bring our ideas together. Our gigantic numbers would make a great ally.

There is no compassion for the non smoking rule. How many owners of bars and restaurant establishments have managed them all their lives? There is no mercy? Many have to close shop and into question come why there isn't a N.O.R. for them to belong. These small businesses are taking the bite.

Let's do this. Let's take the perquisites away from our politicians and see how long they survive. After all they only work a little over hundred days a year and vote themselves raises periodically. I'm sure they've never bought their own tissue paper. Multi-million dollars are spent on perqs. for our politicians. What shame for them to accept.

Life is full of surprises. Little did we know or even think of belonging to an association that is humongous in structure. This is special. Opportunity is welcoming present business people and new start up businesses with a network stabilizing their environment.

Tax money allocated to universities that set up businesses to compete with the "Mom and Pop Stores" is ludicrous. These universities have become financial institutions no longer an inspiring place for higher learning. The credibility of achieving knowledge is fine; however, are the students getting the education they deserve for the amount of money being paid? Universities and colleges have been overtaken by greed or super capitalism.

Thinking of starting your own shop may not be as secure as it once was. However, unification may be the vital anchor. A business person can no longer take the necessary management ship the full course. Government intervention seems to find a way to block the waterway.

In this time of globalization, support is inevitably needed for every individual acting alone in stores everywhere. Giving owners of small business a chance to incorporate in a unit of enormous proportions is a necessitation. Shedding a light of hope deeply desired, paving the way to conquer present problems and coming up with solutions before new obstacles exist, is a goal within reach.

Problems by lawmakers are all that has been offered. Yet, an association would enhance and glamorize our body of members by solving one problem after another and not let any new problems control our destination. While the government faces new problems our focus will be on remedies, remedies and more remedies.

Government should have no control over businesses. Take the minimum wage. If it is constitutional, then employers deserve compensation. Does government have the right to tell small businesses how much to pay their employees? Do they have the right to tell people when and where to smoke? Our forefathers never had this in mind. The country was built on many freedoms that have lost their validity in today's world.

Take a look at what the government has done to the ideas put in motion by one of the greatest Presidents ever. They have taken most of

President F. D. Roosevelt's ideas and obstructed them. The rest speaks for itself.

The repetition of the need for national health care has been repeated continuously. At present national health care would not be feasible; thus, becoming another obstacle for small business.

Remedy + Repetition = Reward—In other words, we all know the problems. It's the process of solving the problems that need repeated. The energy must be channeled to serve the people by presenting and implementing ideas that work for everyone. Every problem must be addressed as it appears. Solving an issue fifty years later could be detrimental.

Our repetition will be answers that work so every problem and many future problems are solved before they appear. An idealized scenario: The reality is simply authentic unraveling.

Can we do that? Yes, a National Organization of Retailers will channel all its energy into workable and achievable goals as they appear for the welfare of all.

The country's national leaders feel that decreasing the national deficit is to create more debts. Wow, retailers know better than that. Entrepreneurs running a business with this type of logic would be bankrupt in no time.

Retailers would solve something before it becomes too hard to deal with. If our country had the likes of Warren Buffet and Bill Gates as its leaders, then maybe all financial issues would disappear by their mere presents. Congress is made up of mostly lawyers. As business people very few would be successful in business with their logic.

One thing for sure is that small business has the potential of becoming a major factor in the welfare of their destination by uniting together as one.

Priority—Group Achievement:

Unification can administer for the business landscape what shop owners cannot achieve individually. A National Organization of Retailers across the nation with its leadership supported exclusively by small-business owners is needed. That's important.

From all indications there are 10-20 million small businesses (depending on your sources) that employ most of the work force. Half of these businesses have fewer than 30 employees and become the target for a N. O. R.; thus, the organization would easily cover millions of employers.

Independent businesses that take in less than $500 thousand a year are usually struggling. Most medium and large sized businesses are not in the shoestring lurch day-by-day survival. Many retailers suffer major setbacks that can be clarified by one word—unite.

It should be evident that small business whether right or wrong has no defense when going against any tax entities. Fortunately, I have always been right, but question myself as to what would happen if being wrong. And you think terrorism is scary.

Having a network would be the best thing that could ever happen to owners of small business. One cannot do it alone. We are unappreciated in our contributions for the betterment of society. A powerful defense mechanism is urgent to end power abusers. Our American Dream has turned chaotic. We are in a position to bring back the American Dream in all its glory.

Entrepreneurs talk the talk. Now, we must walk the walk. The following summary put in motion will walk the walk. There are no sidesteps in this scenario.

Summary
1. **Unite**—National Organization of Retailers
2. Appoint **leaders** to govern the association
3. Select **lobbyists**—representation
4. Develop **Base Structures**—one for each element
5. Build a **Support System**
6. **Family**—all family time 24/7 is quality time
7. **Integrity**—N. O. R. built on ethics, compassion and understanding.
8. Reward **hard work** and **honesty**
9. Progress—make all positive changes for the **longevity**
10. Motto: **Remedy + Repetition = Reward**

Due to the seriousness of this manuscript, a brief pause is suggested.

Why One Shouldn't Eat Pancakes for Breakfast

One shouldn't eat pancakes for breakfast because it will weight one down all day. You will be hobbling instead of walking when going from place to place.

When you sit down, it will be hard getting up and you might need support. If the pancakes shift to one side, you could tip over and fall.

Being too full to eat, when dinner time comes one will just piece away at the food. Watching a sports game you won't sit and rise as quickly as the other cheering fans.

By bedtime the pancakes have worn off and you will toss and turn all night. That is why one should eat pancakes before going to bed. They will weight one down and you won't shift while sleeping.

CHAPTER 7

POLITICAL BASE STRUCTURE

Due to the fact that all small businesses have absolutely no representation whatsoever in Washington D. C., entrepreneurs remain drowning in an ocean full of sharks. One by one, owners of small business are going bankrupt or closing shop because there is not enough income to support a family, let alone provide health care or funds to put aside for a family's college education. Almost all of these hard working and honest retailers are working eighty hours per week without any sort of help from the government. At the end of these exhausting days, there is little gratification for their labor.

Small-business owners and their future constituents are made up of millions of people operating separately. Because of this, small business' size works against, rather than for itself. The small businesses in America have helped to form the backbone of this nation's prolific economy. However, without a central organization, this huge and diverse group is virtually voiceless in the political arena.

Small business has the potential to become a political authority, setting the economic trend. It is becoming more and more apparent that a N.O.R. would help to solve a great deal of the problems facing small businesses.

Opportunities cannot materialize without a plan. A strategy must be devised toward the higher standards of real economic growth that emphasizes the development of an employer and employee's potential. The advancement of productivity is marred by government intervention with their unproductive ideas, rules and regulations. Channeling the concentration toward the individual by supplying compassion, common sense and understanding will pave the way for the opening of many doors never before known.

For too long, retailers have worked diligently to maintain substantial taxes for the government without achieving anything of value for themselves. Entrepreneurs and their employees are a large portion of the taxpaying work force, yet it is they who the government has been the most reluctant to help.

Credible evidence cannot be found supporting the theory that current economic ideas are in tune with the success of small business management. The government's irrational ideas keep the atmosphere in shambles. Inexperienced to small businesses' needs lawmakers are incapable of setting standards that are effective and ethical.

Legislators' jobs require that they live for the day while letting others deal with tomorrow. The results are very often a series of quick-fix programs that are the equivalent of using a band-aid to close open-heart surgery.

An example of this is the tobacco law that was passed in February of 1997. Millions of clerk across the country have to I. D. people wishing to buy cigarettes. Checking the I. D. of anyone who appears to be under 26 in order to sell them cigarettes is ludicrous. What has been accomplished? According to teens under the age of eighteen, "It just takes five minutes longer to get our cigarettes." Duh! And, yet, the beat goes on—entrap retailers. Having little interest in the future development of society's small business sector, legislators leave business people looking for assurance, constructive support, and guidance elsewhere.

In the early 1960's President John F. Kennedy understood what was needed for the survival and continued growth of all business. His progressive policies helped move the nation forward into a new era of economic growth and development. These included acts like slashing the federal income tax across the board; thus, he was able to assist all the people, rich as well as poor, who were repressed financially.

The Kennedy economic ideal called for money to be distributed directly to the taxpayer, thus giving them more direct cash flow. This cash influx served as a powerful force to spur the economy. With that type of help, the extra money that merchants had been spending to pay the government was geared toward hiring new employees and expanding the business inventory. America was saved from hard times, and the newly created jobs allowed the economy to grow and the nation to prosper. Such a bold move would be virtually inconceivable in today's archaic and antiquated mode of government. However, if such a program were implemented, the result would likely be similar to its 1960's predecessor.

For Congress to reach its full potential, a business leader as well as leaders from other occupations must come forward in every sector in life. This would provide equal protection for everyone. It may sound silly at first, but how much sense does it make for America's governing body to mostly come from essentially the same profession? With most members of Congress being lawyers, it is highly improbable for them to remain in touch with the thoughts and concerns of most of the country's work force.

The House of Representatives and Senate have consistently proven this theory to be true, as they have repeatedly granted themselves raises while the standard of living for most American retailers has diminished.

Rhetoric without adequate action leads nowhere. The descent occurs because of wasted time spent on proving one's opponent wrong rather than working with them to find a solution to the real problems facing Americans. This descent also occurs when one member states facts that each member of Congress displays no knowledge or talent of researching.

C-Span may offer some of the most amusing and fictional entertainment on television. Just before they slam each other senseless, one can hear others using words and phrases such as "The Honorable Delegate" and "Mr. Chairperson". The results can be quite comical. Some debates border on Abbott and Costello's famous "Who's on First?" comedy routine. Much is said, little is understood and nothing is resolved. They bring to mind thespians, acting out a satirical version of a script based upon *Robert's Rules of Order*, which is the official set of rules for correct parliamentary procedure.

Time is of the essence as the world turns quickly.

That's the way it is!

The New Proposal is as Follows:

Lobbyists are needed in Washington D. C. to represent and pursue the same benefits for the small business communities that are enjoyed by the other professional associations throughout America. If the government is willing to regulate entrepreneurs, it also must be willing to help them. There is plenty of precedent here. Taxation without representation has long been a major political bone of contention. No assistance has been offered; therefore, retailers are in the lurch and must set up their own standards.

With a National Organization of Retailers task force of field representatives in place, the organization can get a better feel for what is needed and wished for by the association's members. Lobbyists can convey our messages. The following list can be compiled quickly and accurately via computerized systems.

PROPOSED GRIEVANCES:

1. Guaranteed wage for employers with five or more employees: Many employers make less than minimum wage; therefore, when the government raises the minimum wage, they must reimburse the employer. The solution for minimum wage is to lower taxes. Let government feed into the paychecks. N.O.R./Congress

2. Health Insurance-Medical Care: Depending on the new health care system being implemented, a better program may be needed for small businesses. N.O.R.

3. Dental Insurance: Dental care must be provided for the whole family. N.O.R. would cover 70% of all dental bills. N.O.R.

4. Eye Care: Eye care must also be provided for the whole family. N.O.R. would cover 50% of all optometrist bills. N.O.R.

5. Taxes must be lowered according to the wages that are earned, and taxes must be lowered to meet the needs of small business. This requirement would leave extra money for entrepreneurs to build their businesses to a new level. N.O.R./Congress

6. There should be no income tax on the first $25,000 earned. This measure would also give small business the extra boost needed to advance financially. N.O.R./Congress

7. No payments should have to be made in advance for an employer's federal quarterly tax return on employees or

employer's federal annual return. Book work, energy, time and postage are only a few of the unnecessary problems created by legislators that need to be eliminated. This would allow business people extra cash to work with throughout the year. N.O.R./Congress

8. In case of an honest mistake in filing any tax return, it is necessary to have a period of adjustment without any assessment levied. The labor relation lobbyists would become effective in being the mediator or arbitrator. N.O.R./Congress

9. A solid retirement agenda: We need a retirement program that is more effective than the present Social Security plan. This could be achieved by structuring a retirement program in much the same way as the National Education Association's retirement system. N.O.R.

10. Aid to employers should be offered in the form of grants. Grants set up by the N.O.R. to further enhance the business sector of society would be to encourage management to be more productive. If Congress wants to issue grants to small business, then so be it. I have no problem with this. Consequently, if they want to offer grants in the form of loans to be paid back with interest, then a new debt has occurred. N.O.R.

11. We need paid sick leave. This deserves a lot of discussion, and may fall under the health care plan. Currently, most merchants work through their illnesses because they have no other choice. All factors must come into play. N.O.R.

12. We need financial assistance for employee job training, and it is felt that Congress should issue this money. The inadequate individual who leaves his or her job within a short period of time through no fault of the employer has created a financial burden to merchant. Congress

13. Funds need to be set up for family member's college education. Mutually set up by the N.O.R. for family members wishing to attend a university. N.O.R.

14. Congress to return money to small businesses in proportion to the sum allocated to education, technology, defense and government—federal, state and local.

15. We need to have insurance for disaster relief. The small-business person needs to be compensated in the event of an unexpected disaster. N.O.R./Congress

16. Banks should be responsible for customers' bounced checks. Any and all products that the banks issue would be the responsibility of the banks. Financial institutions should not charge for overdrafts within a certain time period when deposits are consistent. N.O.R.

17. Honesty and integrity, exemplified, need no explanation. In the N.O.R., every decision would be technically based on ethics, trust and good faith.

The branching out of small businesses to form a large segment of the economy through a N.O.R. is vital to gain access and representation in Washington D.C.

Falling prey to political manipulation can no longer be tolerated. Grouping together will give retailers an advantage with politicians, especially when they are running for office. What goes around comes around. Enduring political unfairness or broken promises has small business in a lurch. Comical in its stature politicians display arrogance as they inwardly laugh when making promises.

Focusing on honesty, ethics and integrity, N.O.R. will be the agents of optimism, creating a positive and assuring direction with significant changes. Entrepreneurs cannot assist others until provisions are made in solving their own problems. Designating the implementation of the remedies can instill great hope in the reality of a renewed American Dream. The rebirth of the dream will be beneficial to everyone.

Let's do it! We have the capacity to make this the best generation of business people on the globe. As the N.O.R. grows, the superiority of entrepreneurs across America will grow in a fashion beyond our wildest dreams. Wisdom, our knowledge that has already surfaced, along with patience while gaining experience and discipline to gauge our direction, are qualities to be endured.

It is important that members use the resources afforded by a N.O.R. in order to achieve the accomplishments that cannot be perceived by acting alone. The adversaries that have incited us to anger have now brought us together so owners of shops can dedicate themselves to a prominent fulfillment of excellence and a progressive future of ample substance.

The period of ownership in the past will be lengthened to an era of tranquility and prosperity. A retailers' association shall reinstate the American Dream. N.O.R. will focus on matters of stress and strain while the leadership of small business will enjoy the new events that are shaping the true meaning of capitalism. In numbers we will grow to new heights.

N.O.R. could not possibly work within the guidelines of the present Congress. Until our government leaders seek reform (a workable agenda) toward small business, we cannot subject our association to their structure. The separation of N.O.R. and Congress continues. The dissension that has occurred in the past will be open for future discussions but only in terms of remedies. If there is a solution to any retailer's problems with the legislators, we will proceed in a professional, orderly and constructive manner to find it.

As ordinary people we sincerely want to equal the wealth and provide a home for the family and not merely a house. With one vital point in mind, how many families sit down at the dinner table together and have meals on a daily basis? The importance of this question must be addressed for many reasons.

Remedy + Repetition = Reward

A third party must enter the scope of America's current political landscape if we are to avoid dissension and further fragmentation of our nation along lines of political corruption. The preservation of democracy must be accorded a move away from the current two party system so that we, as a country, may better serve the interests of every man, woman and child living under the flag of the United States of America. The poor families left behind in a prosperous society must be solved with compassion and sincerity, displayed by the likes of President Franklin D. Roosevelt.

We must realize the mistake of today's feigned political ignorance to the plight of citizens of less than fortunate circumstance and bring them under the rule of a just political entity elected by the voice of the people. Under the current system that articulation does not necessarily exist. A third party would serve as a realization of that proclamation, providing Americans with new choice. No American should have to vote their apathy for a candidate simply because they believe it to be the choice of the lesser evil, for if that is the case, evil still holds office, regardless of the degree it takes.

Positive vision from the greatest house in the country must be projected with trust and insight as to the perspective and wishes of the entire nation's inhabitants especially where the darkness shows no signs of light. There is no greater passion than the enthusiasm of humanistic values over materialistic possessions that exceed the maximum value. Until this voice is heard, owners of small businesses will have to balance the equation by organizing an association that fits the desires of all its members.

I strongly feel in a two party system, an issue should be brought before Congress by a mix of several individuals from each party, and each member represent the people and not the political party in which they were elected. Once the idea is presented to Congress as a two party piece of legislation, then a determination of a valid solution should be voted upon. If the piece of legislation is voted against, then the necessary and proper justified changes must be inserted until the proposal is met with approval. Party affiliation when voting for the passage of a bill of immeasurable importance must not be a factor; thus, support for the people will achieve a unified government.

Bailout by the government for mismanaged insurance, bank and auto industries is a term that merchants cannot relate to. It's called bankruptcy. Stealing from the poor and giving to the rich is not the American Dream. Yet millions of jobs in small business are lost every year. More lies by politicians, time to bailout big corporations in order to survive, do not match a resilience nation financially.

A classic statement at the hearings for the three major car companies in November of 2008 has America historical. One Senator told one of the CEOs, who all flew into Washington D. C. on their own big corporate private jets, to sell it and schedule a commercial flight back to Detroit. Remedy: Stop overspending, the root of the problem. One wonders, who hired the idiots?

Congress has every reason to believe bailouts will be mismanaged. However, they seemed to ignore incompetence. Is that because our leaders themselves are incompetent? Financial mismanagement at universities will need a bailout eventually. Universities are another case of financial abuse. Why does Congress think bailouts won't be mismanaged? Again, the tax money needed for owners of small business is financing more luxuries enhancing the rich.

Greed has overtaken capitalism. If a downward path of greed continues spiraling, then many will feel the depths of derogation. There must be a better solution. Cleaning house of all executives, hiring new authorities with lesser pay, no perqs. and no bonuses sounds like a great start.

The American Dream is in your sleep, but once you awaken its reality is an American Nightmare. **In order for small business to stay alive until an organization is established, we must form an alliance with America's working associations.**

Our alliance must operate and merge with associations in other occupations such as: teachers, lawyers, doctors, plumbers, electricians, police, firefighters, nurses, along with all workers of the private sector to vote as a group for political leaders. A person who walks the walk instead of sidestepping rhetoric could be a healthy change for our society.

By applying ethically the traits of capitalism small businesses could provide an accurate image as to the people's needs before everyone has lost their jobs. Small Business is going to get washed up with Washington politics, power and greed. Our time is <u>now</u>.

Corporate greed in the political system has extraneous governors in some states trying to dismantle workers' Unions and Collective Bargaining. Wisconsin's private sectors in April, 2011 are protesting against their newly elected Republican governor who is trying to take away worker's rights.

Unions and Collective Bargaining started in Wisconsin about eight decades ago and became effective in 1959 to give laborers a chance to be heard. Unions and Collective Bargaining form the foundation that holds the country together.

Republican governors are trying to annihilate workers rights because ninety-two percent of all financial donations from labor are given to Democrats. Republicans rationalize, saying it's the budget. **That's fraud.**

It is a national movement by the greedy, obsessive Republican governor of Wisconsin and Republican governors of other states who want to end Unions and Collective Bargaining. Mean spirited politicians are against progressive unions that are laborers' hope. Supporting corporate greed our political system is not only anti-small business but also labor. Does this remind one of the falls of other nations?

America's new heroes are the fourteen Democrat Senators that left the state of Wisconsin to delay the voting on the issue of dismantling Unions and Collective Bargaining.

Collective Bargaining is the best way to resolve disputes. Could a political act to silence workers be about greed and selfishness? Reducing the security of laborer's rights by busting their Unions and Collective Bargaining is a Republican dream demeaning the political process.

The fourteen Senators loyalty to the workers who voted for them is unsurpassed. What they have accomplished in three weeks is for the good of the country.

It's sad they had to leave their families to accomplish their goal, but I'm sure these State Senators and their families will gain positive recognition

The good Senators in Wisconsin along with Ed Schultz of "The Ed Show" and labor protesters are the only defense the public has. Hopefully more will join as the protests go forward.

Power and Greed

The politics of power and greed are destroying this country if they haven't already. Dismantling Unions and Collective Bargaining, Ohio State Bill 5 has many political leaders abusing their power to satisfy greedy billionaire campaign contributors. While leaders have a spending addiction and depend on corrupt money to support their habits, they would be most wise to enter a spending addiction rehab.

If you or I pollute the ocean with a tissue, we are given a fine and maybe a jail sentence. Yet, what happened to British Petroleum causing the oil spill in the ocean? They were slapped with a wet noodle.

A well spoken and brilliant Oscar winner, Charles Ferguson, on the night of the Academy Awards said in his acceptance speech, "—that three years after a horrify financial crisis caused by massive fraud, not a single financial executive has gone to jail. And that's wrong." The statement rings true.

Greed destroyed countries many years ago, Iraq a decade ago, lately Egypt and Libya and other countries will fall in the future. Let's hope America isn't in the mix.

Protecting the future for what America stands for is not only the goal but our obligation to preserve why our forefathers came to this country. While most Americans are struggling just to put food on the table, Wall Street financed by the billionaires is having a banner year. If we let greed overtake this country, then we too will fall. Although, America is resilient, it cannot sustain unbridled greed.

Many leaders are as incompetent as the past CEOs of Goldman Sachs and Bear Stearns. Wonder how the credit bureaus rate states and the nation. If their rank is anything above a zero, then the validity of credit bureaus is highly dubious.

Owners of small business must seek resolutions not revolutions. We need cooperative leaders who support genuine worker's rights. Governors trying to bully workers, if successful, in all probability will cause the nation to meet the same fate as Egypt and Libya and the United States has a long history of legal violence against organized labor.

The wrong path our country has chosen is not only a bad sign, but the politicians keep digging the hole deeper. Their strategy for coordinating income and expenses simply does not work.

In order to balance the budget, you spend only what you take in; thus, keeping assets ahead of expenses is most gratifying. The depression is getting worse each day taking small businesses to a new lower level. The political system no longer works for the majority.

After departing office in 2000, President Clinton's legacy of peace and leaving America with a financial surplus was awesome. However, his legacies have been on an eleven year downward spiral, leaving many in despair. Politicians of corruption who are eliminating worker's rights must go. Leaders do not know what school teachers are all about in today's society. Educators are also fulfilling parental guidance (hence the Latin phrase, *in loc parentis*); therefore, performing double duty which is more of a challenge than educators had expected. They teach and inspire students in areas where the father and mother have neglected.

Teachers earn every penny they make and every benefit they are given. The teachers and college professors are the inspiration that makes America what it is today. If the governors would walk in the shoes of school teachers just one day, they would probably faint from exhaustion. If they walked in the shoes of employers across the nation, they couldn't stand the idea of no pay at the end of the day.

Unions and Collective Bargaining are the strength that has held this country together. Bargaining enhances rational behavior, and not the irrational behavior of power happy politicians. The evil leaders must be recalled and put out of office before dictatorship rules.

I honestly hope this book will give owners of small business and their workers the inspiration to join together with not only themselves but with other associations to save the working class. Crushing the American Dream is a sign that America has to make changes, and those changes are ones politicians are unable to address

The teachers and all other workers are not getting the needed support from the Democratic Party. Other options are in demand, because America's public service workers will be confused as who to vote for in the next election since many Democrat politicians are not walking the walk.

Legalizing Unions and Collective bargaining in 1959, Wisconsin became the first state to honor worker's rights. Now the Wisconsin Republicans want to crush the backbone of the economy by destroying those rights.

We can no longer depend on legislatures to protect the rights of workers. Therefore, we have to do research to find the likes of Presidents Washington, Jefferson, Lincoln, F. D. Roosevelt and Clinton. We need any one of these brilliant and well meaning presidents now. They not only walked the walk, but President Clinton jogged the walk. That's even better!

If you're gonna' talk the talk you better walk the walk. These Presidents of great foresight were an inspiration to all. They had no evil aspirations.

Leaders have made it more reasonable for all associations to amalgamate and fight dictator's doctrines to keep America sound. A third party of unity and compassion is an option for consideration.

When you say you are cutting the budget, then why does government's deficit and debt keep going up? It could be that I've got the wrong definition of budget, but I don't think so.

Our present leaders in Washington D.C. didn't walk the walk for hard working people. Promises are just manipulation to get the vote. Giving a bad name to rhetoric by not walking the walk would not settle with genuine orators of the past.

When we hear politicians saying they are running to make a change, we better ask if it's a change for the better or worse. It's important to define the word change. We've got to get this country working for all of us and quit feeding into **mismanagement, the culprit.**

We deserve a government that works for all the people. We need a better America. The country oriented on greed seems incapable of helping the poor and middle class.

It's time to dismantle greed. It's time to disassemble the leaders of corruption. It's time to give Social Security recipients their cost of living raise. Greed is a gigantic force and Satan's forces are on the rise.

The country needs a God of Good not idiots of evil. Our leaders want to lower taxes on corporations and tax everyone else including Girl Scout cookies, the Boy Scout popcorn fund and less spending at children's hospitals.

Democracy is the theory that people know what they want and is assured they will get it

The whole world is watching as money is being shifted from middle class Americans to the billionaires who financed crooked politicians' campaigns. Evildoers have no limits.

The youth, educated and unemployed started the protesting in Egypt. The fact that 1% of the country had most of the wealth was another reason. Does that sound familiar? As always good will prevail.

Food and shelter money was deprived when Social Security recipients didn't get their cost of living raise in the past two years. Therefore picking on the elders, is just as bad as shifting the money. The elderly paid their dues and earned every bit of their retirement money.

There seems to be a lack of conviction. Communications are lacking between dictators and the citizens they represent. This comes as no surprise since dictators are incapable of listening. That's why they are called dictators

An owner of small business' whole itinerary is priceless when it involves interaction with the public on a daily basis. Communications with the public on a sincere and honest standard levels the bar. The interaction is called speak and listen. These discussions give everyone a chance to be heard.

Listening to the voices of the public on an informal basis gives the self-employed notions that help develop innovations. New creations keep the business successful. Intercommunications suggest if politicians do not run a country within their means, it puts the whole country at risk.

We don't need political intervention in small business. Many people have left the country, and the United States needs them back. In our two party systems Democrats and Republicans alike have made a mockery of our democracy. Has greed warped their sense of humanity?

A National Organization of Retailers and their counterparts must amalgamate to make America the dream it once was. The only thing needing dismantled is corporation monopolies and all the politicians that cater to them.

The ace in the hole is our <u>strength in numbers</u>. **To eradicate the American Nightmare is to bring into being the American Dream.**

CHAPTER 8

RETIREMENT BASE STRUCTURE

For all practical purposes, Congress has neatly eviscerated President Franklin Delano Roosevelt's Social Security dream of a retirement plan for the elderly, which would insure their financial security, as well as their privacy. When the program was in its infancy, Social Security numbers were used to help allocate funds to individual recipients. Social Security numbers were not issued as an alternate form of identification for privacy invasion. This has, of course, changed over time. It is now common for Social Security numbers to be used as just that. Changing the rules in the middle of the game is wrong. For all of Roosevelt's contributions to set aside money for a sound retirement fund, especially for low-income families, his volumes of paper work have been hit with an extreme and decreasing volatility.

The following will be discussed:
1. Privatizing Social Security
2. Solutions to a sound program
3. Other options
4. Implementing a retailer's retirement fund

Privatizing Social Security:

If the privatizing of Social Security is played out allowing workers to invest a portion of their paycheck in whichever way they see fit, Congress may find this to have catastrophic consequences on the financial destiny of senior citizens. The impact of privatization in Social Security reform would be devastating. I realize that the economic status of individuals paying into Social Security today leaves a lot to be desired, but private investment has proven to be detrimental in numerous cases.

Many investors lost their retirement funds to company scams within the New York Stock Exchange. A lot of older individuals invested in Lucent Technology losing practically all their Social Security payments to date. Enron Corporation's corruption produced millions of dollars for its leaders, leaving the company bankrupt and many 401k investors flat broke.

It is true that some individuals would prosper from such a reform in Social Security, but we cannot in good conscience sacrifice the good fortune of a few to cloud the issue of inequality that would be raised by such a measure. The Social Security System was established for poor people. Upon retiring they would have an income to financially help them through the rest of their lives.

Solutions to a sound program:

Solutions to the problem would NOT be to move the eligibility age to draw Social Security payments up a couple of years, nor would it be advisable to move the full percentage paid into Social Security from the first $106,800 of an employee's paycheck higher than 15.3% (employee pays 7.65% into Social Security and Medicare while the employer equals the 7.65%), nor would it be commendable lowering amounts already being paid to individuals who have made an honest living.

Setbacks of any retirement money would jeopardize the whole economy because the spending would be less. Less spending means lost jobs. This is exactly what happened. Cost of living for Social Security recipients were not given in 2010 and 2011. Many small businesses saw less spending. Someone tell our legislatures this is how trickling down works.

Other Options:

A few simple reform ideas that would work in the long run enable the elderly to be happy for the rest of their lives are as follows:

1. Stipulations need to be made stating that Congress can no longer dip into the coffers of Social Security and Medicare funds when money is needed for other governmental ventures. No exemptions for other governmental entities can be granted in order for this program to work effectively and with longevity.

2. Pay back the money taken from the system in the years past. Spending other people's money in this peculiar incident is thievery.

3. Taxing individuals two to four percent on what they make over the drop off point in 2010 of $106,800 would immeasurably increase the Social Security pot.

4. The Social Security Administration has a union. Why is this necessary? It is not. Eliminate the union within the system. Social Security, Medicare and Income Tax are seeing individual contributions in top-notch amounts because of the excess tax money the high paying jobs technology has created.

If Washington cannot manage money under these conditions of the 90s and now in the new millennium, how do they expect privatizing to function effectively?

Personally, President Roosevelt would not see low income Americans managing their money any better in the new economy, old economy or the new-old economy than they would have over sixty years ago. Overhauling the system is far more appropriate because Americans must oversee investments for their children's future, adult education, foreseen or unforeseen medical expenses, vacations, luxuries and family upkeep. Therefore allowing people to make their own investments towards retirement may allow people the unfortunate ability to place all their eggs in one basket and risk losing everything.

Unless Congress acts responsibly, it may eradicate a superior program that was developed by one of the greatest men in the twentieth century. A man of compassion and sensitive to elders solved a need of those less fortunate.

Congress has only focused on stating a problem does exist, without presenting any workable solutions whatsoever. Solutions, solutions and solutions are where the focus needs to be.

Implementing a retirement fund within a N.O.R:

Regardless of how the retirement fund is handled, we must understand that it's one of the only benefits that merchants and their employees can rely on. It is because of uncertainty that the National Organization of Retailers cannot deny the fact that a retirement program for shop owners is very much needed and must be added as a base structure in the agenda until we are sure Social Security is here to stay.

Whether it is voluntary or mandatory, implementing a retirement plan is another top priority in the association. If the National Education Association can put together an effective plan, then there is no reason our organization couldn't successfully enact some forming of pension to rely on.

Because of the confusion in Congress concerning the retirement fund, we must have other options. A retirement program would entail contributions from members to be invested in funds with high returns overseen by the N.O.R. leaders. A financial plan for businesses that do not survive can achieve benefits for the retailer according to one's contributions while in business.

Again, each structure must be fashioned properly and updated when needed, so not to become archaic. Applied ethics and compassion would be the workable foundation of a sufficient plan to accommodate all the members.

Individuals receiving Social Security benefits designated that they were pleased with the system. However, they were dissatisfied while paying into the program because of mistrust stemming from rumors that Social Security was running low on funds, and beneficiaries may not reap the rewards. Appling energy to seek constructive remedies would be more rewarding instead of the repetitious problem that Congress seems incapable of providing a solution.

Amazing was the fact that Social Security cards stated: For Social Security purpose—not for identification. President Roosevelt had the unusual foresight and an ability to use his knowledge to help all the people. He limited the use of the number for fear of private information being exploited. Pres. Roosevelt was a man of vision. This appears to be the difference between great innovators and leaders of less quality.

Remedy + Repetition = Reward

The N.O.R. practicing F.D.R.'s vision would be worthwhile in order to accommodate the theory of solutions before the problems arise. Once remedies without perspective are diminished then the whole methodology is meaningless. Therefore, the impact of superb foresight must be delicately governed in a way that few, if any, modifications would be needed by future generations. An excellently thought-out N.O.R. law will reign supreme and not be tinkered with by future leaders.

Meanwhile, politicians' broken promises have hurt millions of individuals. After the election of 2004, finance reform, Social Security or universal health care program isn't heard again until 2008 and in 2012. These problems were handled the same in the last fifty or more years.

Legislation related to these high profile causes did not pass partially due to the inability of elected officials to compromise and group together. Their party-pride was more important than the millions of individuals who are affected by not passing the different issues. However, our interest is retirement benefits. At present, immediate remedies to the problems the Social Security System is facing must be analyzed and solved before it rockets off the planet.

Congress cannot settle all the country's problems in the number of days a year they are in session. Talk about dreaming the impossible dream. In all probability one of the many reasons our proposed leaders get very little done keeping our economy and politics shaky?

N.O.R. may be forced to set up their own retirement system for entrepreneurs. The future would look more promising. One only needs to look at the successful retirement plan set up by the National Education Association for all its teachers.

Our alliance could learn a lot from all the mistakes made by our politicians. Problem solving accuracy without blunders would be our priority.

Trying to analysis why the same issues come up when candidates are running for office leads many to believe that politicians are making fun of the people. You may not get Social Security, you don't have health insurance, etc., but we are going to correct all that. They get in office and many get the feeling leaders use these terms loosely. Nothing is ever done about the issues.

A dysfunctional house is driving the middle class to business bankruptcy. Making more and more middle class people poor by Congress' idiotic ideas and by misspending our Social Security tax money is ludicrous. A national association of retailers is necessary to get the respect that has been void for too many years.

Regardless, divided we have nothing. United we can fight back and regain the good business/family life allowing a guaranteed Social Security retirement in the way President Franklin Delano Roosevelt (1933-45) intended.

Congress has not been able to preserve and guarantee Society Security and Medicare. These taxes were forced on working people; therefore, politicians need to show responsibility by addressing the problem. Many problems last forever, because Congress is not in session long enough to accomplish the right solutions.

CHAPTER 9

TAX BASE STRUCTURE

The preparation of a tax structure by N.O.R. requires a lot of studying and patience to create a professional system. It's a matter of entrepreneur technocracy vs. government bureaucracy, or innovation vs. litigation. Certified Public Accountants are vital for the protection of owners of small shops who are faced with numerous tax reports.

These experts are qualified enough to feed a computer information, and will be very helpful in clarifying tax laws on forms retailers must file.

By eliminating the entrepreneur's hours of reading volumes of material to fill out a single tax form, the computer generation will accomplish a new tax goal. This goal is to enhance retailers' knowledge on how to successfully prepare tax forms in less time.

Information would be available for all business people by request. The structure would simplify the knowledge to fill out tax forms. Whenever legislators change or add a new tax bill they complicate matters further. An accountant for N.O.R. would be responsible for alerting the members of any and all changes to their tax laws and forms as soon as these changes occur. A tax up-date would minimize the risk of costly errors when employers fill out forms.

The criteria for the beginning tax base structure has been presented; thus, calming the frustrations of future business owners. Employers are too keyed up, after receiving a tax assessment, to enable an effective response. During discrepancies of any kind, business owners would experience less agony by being notified and not penalized. Noble characteristics such as compassion, understanding and consideration must replace sly acts of greed, harassment, and abuse.

The stress and tension caused by the failure to communicate effectively and constructively can be eliminated by having a tax adjuster from the N.O.R. interacting as a mediator. Rules and guidelines need to be regulated fairly. Just because life is unfair does not mean that we can't make a difference. We don't have to treat human beings unfairly. In fact, if employees of stores treated customers unfairly, the businesses would go bankrupt.

A department for tax discrepancies in the N.O.R. will stabilize the entrepreneur's equilibrium. Tax forms filed late or incorrectly carry an assessment. An assessment is the interest and penalty levied on the merchant, who filed the return in good faith, but according to the tax department an error had occurred. People of business get the penalty regardless. No ethics here, either.

Within the N.O.R.'s tax support system, the chance of the same discrepancy happening a second time can be eliminated, by keeping records of transactions. These discrepancies could be avoided by keeping track of who made what error, and when the mistake occurred. The bookkeeper can call or E-mail in advance of a due date to remind the self-employed person so, the same mistake is not repeated.

In September 1997, the Senate Finance Committee held hearings for three days concerning I.R.S abuse, but that played out as another farce. The Senators with their fingers in their noses and the 'duh' expressions on their faces again illustrates the lack of knowledge the leaders have in our nation. One senator even announced on television that if he answered all the letters sent to him, that's all he would get done. Addressing each letter would be a start in the right direction.

Postmarked or due cannot be emphasized enough. At one time the Bureau for Employment Services in Ohio changed the word 'postmarked' to 'due' on one of its forms. Many months after forms had been sent in; assessment notices started arriving with no explanation. After a year and four notices of $25.00 dollars (adding up to $100.00 dollars because it involved four quarters of the year), the honorable taxpayer satisfied the demand.

It wasn't until the retailer called the tax office that the cause of the problem was revealed. Only a few minutes of communication via the telephone were sufficient for clarification.

Another tax department created an imaginary case by wrongfully and knowingly sending me an assessment for $8,000 dollars. The merchant called the Attorney General's office, and informed them to ignore this notice once it was turned in. However, receiving an assessment from said office was substantial evidence that they weren't listening and acted wrongfully. Hello—is anyone listening?

After the audit was completed the tax department owed me $366.00. A check for $284.00 was received. The anguish, mental strain, sleepless nights and the apprehension that the debt was owed became mind-boggling. It is extremely important for the N.O.R. to assist anyone who has been wrongfully harassed. Vindictiveness was the nature of the problem. Acts of this unfounded assessment are difficult to neglect. As tax departments are rewarded financial payments when errors occur, so should the taxpayer be financially rewarded for mistakes made by tax departments.

An IRS blunder was mentioned in Chapter 5. They wrongfully seized $1,500 dollars from the business account, forcing many nightmares for the small shop owner, only to restore the whole amount three months later. That was an act of injustice. If there was a N.O.R. and it had a tax base structure, the horror stories would not have occurred.

We've all heard our political leaders say there are too much paperwork and too many taxes. Yet, their response is more taxes and added paperwork. How many town meetings does one attend before getting a grip on the business sector and a firm grasp of life?

The trials and tribulations of all the tax departments and small business could be clarified by a base tax structure within a N.O.R. In modern day technology, the only medium through which you can express yourself adequately is an association.

What a shame our country's entrepreneurs had to deal with in all the years of business. The following is a letter sent to two senators in Ohio.

Dear Senator:

I was recently informed about a new policy to help eradicate the epidemic use of cigarettes amongst our nation's under-aged consumers. While I do agree that there is a cause for some concern, I do not agree with the solution to this problem. Punishing the storeowner who sells the cigarettes is shortsighted, misguided, and ineffectual.

This new policy has been implemented because of the government's alleged desire to help this culture's increasingly irresponsible youth. Although it is of noble intention, we cannot continue to make their decisions for them. Decision-making is how we all learn and grow. This is not to say that I, in any way, condone the use of tobacco products by anyone who is not mature enough to make an *intelligent and responsible* decision on the matter. I just don't think that it is up to the small-business owner to help parent the nation's youth. A retailer's job is tough enough without the extra pressure of policing everyone who patronizes his/her store.

If you are truly interested in the health of America's youth, you will help introduce a law that would punish the purchaser and one's parents. A law against possession of tobacco products by *under-aged* persons would be critical in curbing this problem. At present, there is no such law on the books. If you would help pass a law, it would prove that the government's intentions are not to crack down (yet further) on small business, but to combat a growing problem in this country.

I believe in this country; and I believe that people in your position will help your constituents if you can. Public servants have a very difficult job. Their job requires them to pay a great deal of attention to a myriad of different types of people and their problems. In a way, our jobs are not terribly dissimilar. I too, have a job that requires many different skills and abilities. I am sure then that you can relate to how much more difficult your job would be for you if members of the government were to inform you that they were monitoring you for mistakes.

The job of a United States senator requires that he/she sell concepts and ideas in very much the same way my job dictates that I sell an assortment of items. Imagine if you will, members of the government fining or imprisoning you for each time you misspoke or used poor syntax. I'm sure that you would object. That is precisely what is happening to small business owners like myself. The new government *crackdown* is penalizing small businesses far too severely for what amounts to minor mistakes.

There is a growing problem in this country that threatens to destroy everyone from our youth to our elderly. If we don't act soon, every fiber that holds this land together will surely begin to erode. This menacing problem is not *under-aged* smoking. It is far more serious than that. The biggest opponent to unprecedented happiness and prosperity amongst the American people is misguided and poorly conceived governmental interference.

The two Senators responses:

(1)

Thank you for contacting me with your views concerning the involvement of the Food and Drug Administration (FDA) in the regulation of tobacco.

On March 25, and June 21, 1994, the Commissioner of the Food and Drug Administration, Dr. David Kessler, testified before the House Subcommittee on Health and the Environment on whether the FDA should regulate nicotine-containing cigarettes as drugs under the Federal Food, Drug, and Cosmetic Act. In his testimony, Dr. Kessler presented evidence that the tobacco industry had patented technology to manipulate the level of cigarette nicotine content. Under United States Code Section 321 (g) (1), a product is classified as a drug when its manufacturer intends it to bed used to affect the structure of function of the body. Dr. Kessler contends that through the deliberate use of nicotine level manipulation techniques, tobacco manufacturers are undertaking activities that resemble those of pharmaceutical manufacturers and should be considered for regulation by the FDA.

On August 23, 1996 President Clinton announced the final Food and Drug Administration rule to restrict access to and reduce the appeal of tobacco products for children and adolescents, and the agency's proposal to mount a national mass-media campaign on the dangers of tobacco use for young people.

On February 28, 1997, photo identification in the sale of cigarettes or smokeless tobacco for anyone under the age of 27 became required.

Retailers who sell to minors risk penalties of $250 or more. State and local officials now work with FDA to monitor retailers across the country.

Effective August 28, 1997, vending machines or self-service displays are to be prohibited, except in places where no one under age 18 is present. Coupons for these products will no longer be redeemable by mail and no outdoor ads for cigarettes or smokeless tobacco will be allowed within 1,000 feet of a school or public playground. Furthermore, sponsorship of any sporting or any other event, team, or entry identified with a tobacco brand will be authorized; however, sponsorship in the corporate name is permitted.

It is my hope that Congress will continue its support of efforts to protect our children from the harmful effects of tobacco. I appreciate having the benefit of your views on this important matter. Please feel free to contact me again if I can be of any assistance.

----

(2)

Thank you for your letter regarding the Food and Drug Administration's (FDA) regulation of tobacco products. I appreciate hearing your concerns.

I believe we should do everything we can to keep kids from smoking. Tobacco use by children is serious problem and I believe that tobacco companies should not target teenagers in their marketing and sales campaigns.

As you know, the President announced new FDA regulations aimed at stopping teenage smoking. The new regulations target the sale and the advertisement of tobacco products to teenagers by limiting the placement of advertisements and sales. To prevent the sale of tobacco products to teenagers, retailers of those products now must check photographic identification of customers under the age of 27. The FDA also requires the tobacco industry to conduct an educational campaign regarding the health risks associated with tobacco use. Additional regulations will take effect during the summer of 1997.

Once again, thank you for your letter. If you have further concerns, please do not hesitate to contact me.

—To quote church lady, on TV's *Saturday Night Live*, "Now isn't that special?"—

Ban youth smoking—Right!

Penalize retailers for selling, giving or buying cigarettes to anyone less than 18 years of age. Yeah, that 40 page piece of legislation in 1997 doesn't eradicate, but encourages underage smoking.

It is not illegal for minors to buy and use tobacco products. Another blunder! According to federal law enforcement officers cannot touch anyone under age 18 smoking a cigarette.

Politicians unconditionally picking on retailers, and yet taking every bit of tax money they can get are ludicrous. This is a concrete example of Congress working against small business. They just don't get it.

In 2001, the Buckeye State got the graphics right and wrote their own law. A piece of legislation passed in Ohio, on March 15th, 2001 is as follows:

It's already illegal to sell cigarettes, cigars, chewing tobacco or snuff to anyone younger than 18. However, it's not illegal for minors to buy or use tobacco. "Right now, the clerks in the stores can get busted," said Joe Case, a spokesman for the Ohio attorney general's office. Problem was, there wasn't much police could do to the minors who bought tobacco. But beginning Thursday, police will be able to charge them with a crime. Minors will face a $100 fine.

The Food and Drug Administration should be more concerned about child obesity. Home cooked meals are not available with both parents working to make a living. The issue is of major importance. Children are not going to live as long as their parents. Hit the hardest is this generation.

The best love is home cooked meals. Parents monitoring their children's food and where they eat on a daily basis are essential.

The country needs healthy restaurants if the children are always eating away from home. Cafeterias in schools may not be serving the best of foods; therefore, dietitians may be needed to apply the principles of nutrition to diets. The government just doesn't get it.

Small business will need to develop good nutrition for their children. A good breakfast, healthy lunch and a nice home cooked family meal at supper. The goal would be to bring business/family together.

The Food and Drug Administration is measured by their solutions. What has been done to improve the eating habits of children? Obesity is far more dangerous than smoking.

CHAPTER 10

UTILITIES BASE STRUCTURE

Rent Control: Once upon a time a man yearned to establish his own business. His present job could no longer adequately support a wife and two kids. This person, with all the necessary research, had finally put together a portfolio. The lease on the building he desired to rent was $1000 per month for five years.

In those five years the renter had invested thousands of dollars in remodeling expenses and built a gross income of $80,000 a year before taxes. The landlord, sensing his tenant's good fortune, decided to raise his rent for the next five years to a catastrophic $2,500 a month; thus, lowering the merchant's income to $62,000 a year before taxes. All the property in the area had been rented, so there was no place to relocate. In my case the landlord has been fair during the recession and beyond concerning rent of building.

"One man's wages rise is another man's price increase."
—Harold Wilson

An increase of 150 percent for the next five years is unethical. It is improbable the extreme amount could be foreseen; two percent a year would be a more rational increase. No landlord should have vindictive powers over any tenant. Yet, it happened and it has been happening to many merchants. As more landlords take a greedy approach to the American Dream, merchants are having regular nightmares. After

131

building a business at one location, the option to relocate may not look promising.

Future expenses are unpredictable. When increases in business cost occur, (such as ridiculously high rent increase), employer's wages suffer and a new strategy must follow. In this case, the new strategy for survival would be for control of rent and utilities to be set up by the N.O.R. Protection must be arranged to prevent another occurrence of a huge rent increase five years down the line.

Shop owners have been stifled by landlords who take advantage of their tenants with get rich quick schemes, and commissioners who allow exuberant utility increases. We need guarantees. The development of the N.O.R. is needed to block unreasonable rent and utility hikes. Expenses diminish profit. As the store's overhead increases, the small-business owners' paycheck decreases. If businesses were to raise prices on merchandise to cover increased expenses, clientele would leave establishments empty; thus creating another detriment in a no win situation.

Increases in rent, phone, electric, gas, water, sewer and garbage costs are harmful especially in a recession/depression. New rates by the utilities commission are not favorable to small business. All costs may increase the paychecks for utility employees while decreasing the paychecks of the owners of small business.

It is only a matter of time before all of the profit is depleted. The entrepreneur will have to work new avenues for survival in the crucial expectations for their continued existence.

Standards for minimum wage must be worked out in relationship to the employer's income. Consistently giving way to higher rent costs, increased utilities, and a rising minimum wage are diminishing employers' salaries. Our democracy is at stake when small business has to bend over backwards to please others without receiving anything in return. A flaw has developed causing a free enterprise economical hardship to owners of small business.

Because of outrageous utility expenses, chances of surviving a twister are greater than those trying to operate a business successfully. There is an obvious need to pull together to form an association that offers protection for the self employed.

City council members passed a three percent annual rent control. They realized when capitalism turns into greed, all ethics are lost.

Many local government policies affect business directly. Like the federal government, they have very little, if any, experience in business operations. N.O.R. would be capable of influencing local governments

The most intelligent move for the retailer is to purchase land and property. However, if this isn't possible in the beginning, the retailer should look for an establishment suitable for future dwelling. It is possible that a long-term appreciation in property value will produce a greater profit than the business income for the entrepreneur. Do not wait for an opportunity—create the opportunity and feed into its appetite.

The business of an entrepreneur has become much like a trip on the Titanic. The merchant weaves through obstacles, only to inevitably face the big iceberg—government intervention. Figuratively speaking, we are competing with time in a destructible form, with a chunk of frozen water ahead. The development of a National Organization of Retailers can provide the necessary sunshine to melt the adversary and keep the ship afloat. Through unification we can prevent many future business failures keeping our hopes and dreams alive.

Stock adviser Jim Cramer's theory of the United States government, "They know nothing." is pathetic but an awesome discovery.

Governmental interference would be an asset but the reality is they do not research the problem. If companies show no profit, then CEOs and executives deserve reduced paychecks, not added raises, bonuses and more perks.

If owners of small business gave themselves a raise, perquisites and bonuses every year, then bankruptcy becomes the totality. One can only operate on profits. Debts are not good.

Isn't it funny that when government overspends the young have to fit the bill, when corporations have financial difficulty they get bailed out while small business in troubled times is left in the lurch.

How did the backbone of the economy encounter such a dilemma? Is it **Greed**? When the government approved a $700 billion dollar bailout, AIG bank insurers got $250 billion; Thus, Congress saw the money spend in luxuries.

That is all well and good, but at the taxpayer's expense. Robbing Peter isn't an American Dream. It's a nightmare.

Uncomfortably as it is we individually are treated as we let ourselves be. Uniting would see a shift in magnetic proportion for owners of small business.

CHAPTER 11

PRICE CONTROL

Purchasing goods for small business carries a greater wholesale price for items than the cost paid by big corporations. This allows them to lower prices on merchandise sold to customers. Therefore when retailers sell the same goods, competition favors big business. In order to be competitive, individual entrepreneurs deserve the same cost discount that is offered to the larger corporations. Fair trade can be achieved with the development of a N.O.R. The stagnation of small business is much like the bodybuilder who is powerfully addendum free, unable to qualify, let alone win a National Competition Title. Proven true are Shakespeare's words in *Macbeth*: "Fair is foul, and foul is fair."

Consistence in the consistency of inconsistencies involving fair trade has merchants fearing their staying power. Something needs to be changed when retailers must purchase stock from another retail store because it is cheaper than if they would buy goods from the wholesale company. Fair trade becomes an ambiguous term. If an individual retailer purchases in bulk from a wholesaler, stock would consist of only a few items. With limited capital, there would be little or no money for other items.

Under the Federal Anti-trust law there is a provision called the Robinson-Pitman Act, which was enacted in 1936. It prohibited suppliers from giving promotions and price discounts to some businesses and not others. Specifically, it was meant to aid small businesses in receiving the same prices and promotions that larger businesses were already afforded.

That legislation, however, has failed to curb this problem. Price discrimination continues because small-business owners cannot afford the time or money to bring suit to the larger bullies in the market. Government officials turn their heads the other way, as per usual. The fact remains that this problem does exist, and it needs to be corrected. The N.O.R. will have the power and resources to challenge this inequality.

Promotions for products are given to larger chain buyers and worked down the line. These promotions fizzle out before reaching the independently owned stores. Small shops need equal promotions to increase the store's clientele by offering goods at a reasonable price.

The effectiveness of an association is obvious. If small businesses could pull their orders together via organization, they might be offered a lower wholesale price for merchandise. This outcome would be highly beneficial to the merchant. Entrepreneurs need to work together to achieve the ultimate goal of the future American Dream.

If the N.O.R. would provide a price-controlling base structure, the organization could accomplish the same pricing for all purchases from all people. Integrity becomes the potent ingredient that will curb wholesale cost cutting.

Time and time again, one wonders where Congress is. After watching five minutes of C-Span it becomes obvious. As an entrepreneur, one cannot imagine working in the lackadaisical style that is projected on the C-Span screen. One would not be in business five minutes, let alone a lifetime. Congress needs to regroup, regroup and regroup until the world's funniest comedy act gets it together and doesn't forget where they left it. The division between legislators and owners of small business is a huge gap that can only be corrected by the N.O.R.

Our goal is to inform Congress of the desires of retailers, before they inadvertently lead us to bankruptcy. We need to put away our oars and join the ocean liner while the motion is forward. We need equal costs for goods sold to everyone. Eventually, that will create a level-playing surface for the small-business owners.

A support system will be offered with feedback from the merchants. The technical department of the price controlling and promotions agency would handle any misdealing of a promotion.

The promotion of an item will be offered to all businesses, whether the companies voluntarily offer it, or if the N.O.R. has to step in. Every time a company offers a promotion, distributors will notify N.O.R. The association will notify each business owner. N.O.R. will ensure that companies' stock promotions will be offered at the same price to all stores.

Once an organization is established, the price control and promotional staffs will ensure fair play for everyone. The days of playing favorites will no longer exist. Whoever said that life is not fair has not had any experience with the National Organization of Retailers. All is fair. Sometimes the constant repetition of a cliché becomes a gentleman's cop out.

At some point one begins wondering if people just want you out of business, want your money or simply enjoy harassing you by being abusive or all the above. An association of retailers has been needed for years. Entrepreneurs have many unattended needs. It is surprising we made it to the new millennium. Merchants were lucky to make it to the bridge, let alone cross it.

"History will be kind to me; I intend to write it," was eloquently spoken by Sir Winston Churchill. It is with gratitude and genuine feelings that I have written this self help text intended to assist small-business owners from all walks of life. Our dreams for the future are attainable. However, we must unite. If we continue to act alone, the small business landscape of America will be past history. As a National Organization of Retailers we will say it loud and proud—united we stand. I have drawn a plan, and when we follow it and unite, the future will be most kind to all in this 21st century.

Mega stores

Mega stores have put many "Mom and Pop Shops" shops out of business. As the large billionaire stores continue to blossom, many more shops stumble. We must unite. By coming together, our mega-unit will operate as one humongous operation. When we receive the same treatment from wholesalers as the mega stores, our cause will be won. Only then will the free enterprise system be back in full operation. By coming together we can express all of our needs.

"Mom and Pop Owners" owners are faced with another culprit—the Internet. The Internet, with web sites such as "Amazon", "Books-a-million" and "Barnes and

Noble", have already put many bookstores out of business. There isn't a great deal of hope for small business until an association is organized.

The most intimidating to small-business owners are:

1. Government Intervention, which is harmful, instead of helpful.
2. Tax departments, with their abusive behavior.
3. Utilities that constantly rise.
4. Rent control and the devastating increases.
5. Mega stores, which can afford lower prices.
6. The Internet, which allows purchasing on web sites.
7. Banks, with numerous service charges.

Right now we are unprotected and alone when we face any one or all of the above entities. Defense is critical for the defenseless. A N.O.R. can become the necessary protective mechanism that paralyzes the opposition.

Out of the seven troubling sources listed above, the Internet offers a valuable service for the future success of small business. The Internet will be the key in order to organize and unite the country's traditional small businesses. It provides a forum in which to develop our organization.

Aside from being able to organize via the Internet, it also allows another medium through which the members of the association can sell and advertise. Many of our businesses could expand by creating a web site for consumers to purchase goods.

Remedy + Repetition = Reward

CHAPTER 12

LEGAL BASE STRUCTURE

The N.O.R. will have a legal base structure made up of a network of attorneys. A referral system would be available to advise employers of their legal rights in any and all situations. Regional attorneys in the entrepreneur's area would be available to give free consultation when a problem occurs. If additional services would be needed, the merchant would pay 60% of the fee for the attorney or firm. Again, this is a proposal. The percentage would have to be worked out by the N.O.R.

The following terms are used frequently in the law profession:

Litigate: to carry on the trial part of a lawsuit
Implement: to put into effect
Imperative: absolutely necessary or required
Duress: unlawful pressure forcing one to act against will

A business owner should be familiar with these terms before contacting a lawyer in order to understand what is being said.

According to Daniel Oran in his publication of "Law Dictionary for non Lawyers" he states, "The language of law uses mostly English words, but they rarely mean what they seem. Many look like everyday English, but have technical definitions totally different from their ordinary uses. Some contain complex legal ideas compressed into small phrases. Others mean several different things, depending on the area of law, business or politics they come from."

Oran further states his two main purposes for the dictionary: (1) "It attempts to help the reader both understand and use a technical vocabulary;" and (2) "It helps the reader recognize and discard vague, fuzzy words that sound precise and that lawyers often use as if they were precise."

In all business it is better to leave the technical terms and their meanings concerning law to the educated lawyer. Law is a professional career in which you must be certified to practice, and for good reason. An unethical person who has taken a couple courses in law may try to fabricate a false claim against a decent person or business. An activity of this type is usually fraud. When such suits come up against a small-business owner, he or she has limited resources with which to fight the case. This is also true when tax departments try to accuse a person of false or incorrect filing, or when any sort of injustice or discrepancy arises in a small business. We need the assistance of attorneys working on our side. The N.O.R. will be able to provide a network of affordable legal advice that works with and for retailers. A law department will be able to block frivolous cases from going to court, and save the time, money, emotional and mental stress of hard working small-business owners.

There are many classifications where legal assistance may be necessary, such as: consumer protection, will and testimony, liability, domestic, all business and personal interaction or transactions with others, loans and even bankruptcy, just to mention a few. The N.O.R. legal department will have a number for a businessperson to call in order to get advice for a problem in any area.

Lawyers would work in constant proximity with lobbyists. The lobbyists also would be pursuing advice as to the legal procedure and government etiquette for compromising on issues. Attorneys who work with lobbyists would help develop the legal strategies that matter and work for small businesses. Lawyers would be performing numerous duties. Their main course of action would be to handle business lawsuits and give advice to businesspeople on how to stay within the law.

It seems in this day and age suing has become the number one way to gain money for many who are leading financially unsuccessful lives. Few people, if any, can afford the financial burden of a lawsuit. Therefore, a N.O.R. law staff would be a necessity both for business lawsuits and finances.

In the year 2002 no clergy of the Catholic Church could pay the financial price for sexual abuse. These court fines were paid by the church funds. However, justice would be better served if the abused were given counseling by professionals in the field. But as we all know justice is about money. And if money works to cure the ill, then so be it. As a businessperson, I cannot dispute the judge on his decision for justice. I may disagree, but that's it.

However, the problem is with the parents. Parenthood is open communications. Children need the protection, guidance and support of their parents on a 24/7 bases. (No one knows family 24/7 better than country singer and legend Garth Brooks, because that's exactly what he provides for his children). When teenagers cannot talk to their parents concerning any problem, there is a lack of communications.

I am not condoning the actions of the clergy, but feel a serious problem must be settled immediately before it becomes a court case. Parents most often can't afford a crafty lawyer.

If an honorable businessperson is taken to court, he has only the defense he can pay for. This leaves the businessperson at a disadvantage if a slippery plaintiff has the funds for a crafty lawyer who can manipulate the law suit to their advantage.

Let's not fool ourselves. Many times the scales of justice are off-balance. The courtroom is judged by the litigation of the lawyers. If there were a N.O.R. the individual belonged to, he might have an advantage with the aid of a law support system. If a businessperson is wrongfully accused of an unlawful act, it is fine for him to hire an attorney of his choice. However, N.O.R. would be able to provide lawyers who specialize in cases of fraud. A law structure would be beneficial to the members of the N.O.R. in any lawsuit.

Entrepreneurship is booming. With it may be the biggest economic trend in American history. Legal and other support from an association could be the difference between success and failure.

Note: In each base structure, there is offered a short proposal of what is necessary and how it might work. Once the N.O.R. is set up, the organization will be responsible for the technicalities. Their input may prove more valuable and create a better method of workability.

CHAPTER 13

LOBBYISTS

Once a National Organization of Retailers is solidified, lobbyists must be selected to represent the interest and welfare of all members in front of all government entities; federal, state and local. These lobbyists will be entrusted with the duty of conveying the message of our group. Representatives for small-business owners will help forge a new frontier of modern retail in America, strengthening the theory and sound ethic of our motto:

Remedy + Repetition = Reward.

Lobbyists will achieve this agenda through the implementation of a three-pronged system.

1. The first of these prongs will be actual physical representation in Congress and in other governmental departments.
2. The second prong will deal in the involvement of membership to see that members are actively involved, not just people in a crowd. We must collectively share our ideas and opinions without abandon.
3. The third prong is the involvement of all members in terms of financial obligations as well as services rendered on behalf of our organization. This will require us to put in time, energy and work in our respective political communities.

Let's use the following issue as an example handled by lobbyists. Substantial modifications to our tax system could greatly increase the productivity and ease with which we do business.

The basic ideal of these modifications would be a National Sales Tax that would replace all other taxes, and would relieve much of the retailer's heavy burden of bookwork. A system more in league with our state's sales tax procedure, but on a national scale, would accomplish most of these ideals.

Working in constant proximity with Congress, lobbyists acting on behalf of the N.O.R. could provide the seaway needed to help push legislation of this kind through Congress. The resulting elimination of payroll tax duties, tax forms and no tax returns for anyone on April 15th would simplify the process and speed up any tax report, leaving extra time for the family.

In this manner, the N.O.R. would persuade lawmakers to pass legislation favorable to small businesses. The impact would be phenomenal, due to the sizeable membership of retail America. Realizing we are a voice that needs to be heard, Congress would no longer turn their attention elsewhere.

The N.O.R.'s strength must focus on its lobbyists' ability to promote their concerns in government. Still, we must proceed with caution. If politics do indeed breed corruption, then caution is a necessity. We want lobbyists to support our cause with ethics and logic. There are individuals in high places that have achieved their goals without any ethics, whatsoever. We do not relate to this behavior, nor do we condone any unethical antic.

It is not in the best interest of the N.O.R. to intentionally do the wrong thing. In no way will integrity be compromised for cheap gains. It is right to achieve a goal by constructive and positive means, but wrong if it is achieved through a reckless disregard for integrity and ethics. Whether or not tyrants do occasionally achieve esteemed positions is not relevant to our interests.

Though our bicameral system has gone the route of the horse and buggy, we must press on. We must always put family first, with second priority being the business ventures that provide for our welfare. Our goal to restore the American family and reunite them with their community and church is real. That achievement is a trying and exhausting endeavor in this time of political, cultural, moral and social unrest.

I was trained to make life a little easier for anyone and everyone met in my journey on Earth, and to separate myself from individuals of unethical standards. Vindictiveness and a misuse of ethics are mediums of a destructive nature. Negativity must be erased replacing it with compassion and fairness for all.

The business landscape must have a new framework that embraces our country, lest we shall fall into an economic bust worse than 1929 depression. Businessmen typically wear ties to work, and tend to pull at them to loosen the knot when they work very hard or feel pressure. In order to tackle the stress, pressure and obstacles of everyday business today, the retailer must take the tie off completely, in order to get a fresh breath. This tie is everything that is working against the merchant in his business dealings.

Businesswomen must loosen their attire and let their hair run free, for they too face the same challenges as men. With billion dollar mergers taking place, retailers must also merge—not only to survive, but also to strengthen the backbone of our economy, which is small business.

In the first eleven years of the new millennium many middle-class business owners are far worse off than they were as far back as 1980.

The tax money that technology, big corporations and small businesses have accumulated for the government goes beyond its expectations. The credit goes to technology. Yet, over forty-seven million Americans are without health insurance.

However, a health care program would have worked in 1992. But today, it could be harmful to the small business landscape.

Even while retailers open businesses on the web, they still cannot escape the importance of belonging to an association. The Internet will be a strong source in developing a National Organization for Retailers. Entrepreneurs will be able to log on and connect to everyday business being conducted by the group. Up to date information concerning what lobbyists are doing in Washington will also be available.

The lobbyists of other organizations (medical, teachers, etc.) have served their members and verbally fight with representatives of local, state and federal governments to gain what they have today. Their arguments and persuasions with politicians have been so effective it has been comparable to moving mountains. However, these lobbyists must follow the strong ethical standards of the N.O.R. in their dealings with government leaders. Deficient representation would make it highly improbable for the successful longevity of retail shops.

The N.O.R., with lobbyists, will achieve their goals. If Congress is too uncompromising to our ideas, then the entrepreneurs will administrate the needs through the association. Small business is all too familiar with clip joints.

We must work together or else remain chaotic, insecure and ineffective. The totality of entrepreneurial unity would salvage any sinking ship. I'm sure Washington D. C. needs another lobbyist group. Yet, our leaders are the instigators and must be deal with.

Remedy + Repetition = Reward

This theory works with lobbyists when based on ethics, integrity, honesty, unselfishness, understanding and compassion. Spread the wealth more equally. The continuous division of the rich and poor must not be further extended but moved closer together.

If our governors have anything to do with small business, it's almost always negative. They feed into the rich because that is the base the financial base where they get their big contributions.

The American Dream is by its very nature a **risky** business. Our forefathers who emigrated from foreign lands dreamt of building an empire from nothing. The new periodization of the legacy of small business requires a much more substantial amount of money and outside support compared to starting small business years ago.

We must always remember where we want to go, and erase the events of the past that could hamper our success. The mind is like a computer in the sense that deletion is a necessary tool. It must be cleared and cleaned from time to time assuring ample room for new creations. Although failures may be etched in stone, they must leave the mind. Overcoming adversity is the cleanest mind.

Thomas A. Edison visualized longer days, and lit up the nation with his light bulb. Alexander Graham Bell introduced us to long distance vocal communication. Henry Ford expanded the circle of the way we live. Not only did the automobile increase the speed of our lives, it provoked love making mainly in the back seat. The Wright brother's flying machine paved the way for populace jet travel. Television furnished live entertainment, advertisement and news in our homes. In 1969, Neil A. Armstrong and crew in outer space authenticated that "Fly Me to the Moon" was no longer just a song.

Near the end of the 20th century Bill Gates, founded Microsoft, revolutionizing the computer industry. Entrepreneurs must take advantage of the miraculous component and everything that accompanies it. Most profoundly, this means the Internet. Revelations of past prototypes have paved the way for emulations in newer generations. The bottom line of this scenario is innovation.

The business community needs leaders of the above kind to guide us into a more profitable and efficient business environment through the implementation of new technologies and business practices. We must not allow ourselves to become stagnant and reliant on yesterday's tools, but use these devices as steppingstones for the future introduction and development of new ideas.

Owners of small shops, especially the "mom and pop" merchants, need a breakthrough; a support group to help ensure that the American Dream is kept alive.

An integral phase of this group would be lobbyists who represent owners of small business in Congress. These lobbyists could very well be the advocates who would assist in finally bridging the gap that lies between small business and government. Lobbyists would allow our businesses to achieve new frontiers previously unobtainable.

It is necessary that the vital issue of representation must be addressed. Through our organized vote we can better achieve our political agenda. We can force Congress to play by the rules, and promote small business to the congressional priority scale. Our political vote can subvert Congress in just such a position.

An N.O.R. advantage: We'll bring up a predicament and create a solution without being hassled by a bicameral vote. We'll respect the fact that remedies are positively needed for every complication with no problem going unanswered. Therefore, our goal will be to present solutions before dilemmas occur. With our ability to work together and compromise, there seems to be very little reason for conflict. However,

Congress encounters difficulty in passing new legislation as a direct result of a two party system that works in opposition.

President Franklin D. Roosevelt developed Social Security. He foresaw the future of personal privacy on the computer. In the system's development President Roosevelt declared that a Social Security Number was for Social Security Purposes—not for identification; thus, he had it stated on each individual card. Again, Congress created another blunder, and many people are having their privacy invaded through the use of Social Security numbers.

It is ludicrous elected officials in Congress that are destroying the creation by one of the greatest men if not the greatest of the 20th century. Is it any wonder no one cares to vote anymore and the masses are disassociating themselves from politicians? Many lives have added pressure because of the misuse of Social Security Numbers; thus, again, Congress cannot be trusted to act for and serve the people of this fine nation.

One of our greatest freedoms—The Freedom of Privacy (Privacy act of 1974)—has been destroyed. No one has privacy anymore. Even with the lobbyists in Washington D.C., there is evidence that money cannot only influence but determine their way of thinking.

Bribery is beyond the thinking of a N.O.R. Our strategy must only be one of sound ethics in every endeavor. It's not only sound, but also safe. We must have lobbyists in Washington D.C., or small business will remain where it is today—in the pits! Taxation with representation is the American way. This call must be solved.

Business and religion are united and have always interrelated. Furnished with this righteous inspiration gives us not only the ability to think but believe positive. The lobbyists of the N.O.R. will be provided with persuasive, eloquent criticisms to prove their point.

The political logic of our government is complex. If we are to advocate the simplicity, purpose, goal and direction of small business, we must be prepared for a prodigious task. But if we are to do it right, together with the help of N.O.R.'s lobbyists, we will achieve a political, social and economic viability never before seen by the small business community, all while simplifying the entire process. In this sense we really can have a better than fair system. President Clinton knew this all too well.

Tears can no longer be shed for the time of moping has past. By removing intimidation and adversity among ourselves, we will achieve again, what retailers long ago obtained. Staying together, we will survive. Subjecting ourselves to challenges of change by coming and staying together in an N.O.R. with lobbyists is one risk that entrepreneurship cannot avoid. An umbrella of protection has been presented. The decision is now.

Lobbyists must be cautious

Politician's low moral standards have become the den of inequity in an arena that cannot afford moral decay, such as: adultery, child molestation and sex solicitations in public places shattering their political and family lives.

Subjecting our lobbyists to the political structure may present a difficult problem instead of a solution. We do not want to wreck our own families. We cannot afford to have our lobbyists corrupted while trying to put the family/business relationship back together.

Washington D. C. has always been a threat to small business as long as can be remembered. Solving the complications for business lobbyists before they happen is what N.O.R. is all about. It's the good life and entrepreneurs want to keep it that way.

When Larry King (March 7, 2009 Larry King Show) asks Dolly Parton if she would consider a political position, she said, "No". Then he asks her if she would run for president which she said, "they've had enough boobs in the White House".

Remedy + Repetition = Reward

CHAPTER 14

HEALTH BASE STRUCTURES

The development of a health base structure will be a goal unparalleled. Many sectors of society have the opportunity to have health insurance for themselves and their families supported by the taxpayers—those with federal, state and local government jobs. Business owners can no longer depend on a passage of legislation by Congress and must consider an alternative.

The importance of business people in society is crucial and must not go without recognition by being overlooked for health insurance. Financial support from outside sources for entrepreneurs has a minuté chance of gaining momentum; therefore, the N.O.R. is the only resource and possibly the only way to get health insurance. The solution is a health care base structure carried out by the N.O.R. that is affordable and covers all merchants, their families and their employees.

When President Clinton, in his 1992 campaign, said he would legislate, a universal health care program. It didn't happen. What did happen were increased prices of services and medications. Many merchants were forced to discontinue their respective check-ups and needed medication. Congress knew that the health care bill would not pass, but did not prepare the economy to meet the devastating impact on all uninsured business members, and everyone else without health insurance.

What did happen was an unacceptable universal health care program before the legislators, causing doctors to increase their fees, and pharmacies to charge more for prescriptions; thus, creating a triple defeat.

Business people who find health insurance unattainable for whatever reason must persuade the government to allocate money to them for health protection. N.O.R. must consider the matter a serious issue.

The inadequacies of legislators to pass an important piece of legislation have required us to try our own strategy. If the association's lobbyists cannot get Congress to activate a national health care program, then small businesses will have to develop their own plan through the National Organizations of Retailers. Election 2008 had politicians preaching their archaic health care problem. What's new? Solutions are all we want to hear, please.

The worst case scenario would be to ignore health care development and wait for the government to implement a universal health care program. In 1992 it was feasible, but the workings of one today would present a multitude of problems. Beyond the N.O.R will be the State Organization of Retailers (S.O.R.) and Local Organization of Retailers (L.O.R.). These divisions would be helpful in developing proposals for a health care structure in their respective regions.

Until nationwide health care becomes a reality, allocation from the N.O.R. funds is urgent. Insurance for health, dental, vision, hearing and disability is a goal that can no longer be neglected. N.O.R. can enhance employer's welfare and health through unity. However, when it comes to health care, legislation that mandates equality for everyone needs to be passed.

In 2010 Congress approved a National Health Care Program. The program itself is unacceptable, because it's causing more turmoil for small business.

Advancement of civilization: Employers understand N.O.R. is a healthy counterbalance to adversity. Health insurance is a priority that cannot be ignored. Affordable health insurance is vital to gain peace, prosperity and progress in the coming years for entrepreneurs.

Does Washington itself corrupt our leaders, or do they arrive there ill behaved. Regardless, democracy needs to be energized with a system to meet the peoples' urgencies. In the vast age of computerization, fast decision-making and careful planning must emerge. The Democratic and Republican parties are one in the same—dogmatic in their belief. Goals are unapproachable. If Congress is incapable of compromising, an issue like health care reform will have little chance of success.

The members of Congress become quite comical by voting along party lines. They are not in the least charismatic. Conforming to their separate parties has sucked up their individuality; thus, mobilizing the nation basically into two equals. I had always assumed that an issue was brought to the floor for an immediate solution and not a bipartisan vote. The truth is that issues barely pass. It's hard to believe that most issues only pass or fail by one or few votes. Although humorous, it's quite pathetic.

An idea would be to discuss a topic that needs to be handled properly. Then select a committee of Republicans and Democrats. The remedies both parties agree upon will be presented before Congress as ideas from both parties. The issue would be credited to both parties and displaying no party favoritism. For once maybe something constructive can get achieved.

A universal health care program is not a humorous issue for the administration to joke about. Affordable health insurance is a serious venture. A large percentage of employers in this country are struggling for everything they earn. It would be difficult for small business to financially support a health care program. Many entrepreneurs' profit goes to pay taxes to provide luxuries for others, while shop owners cannot afford food and health care for themselves? Think about it. If there is justification for this type of behavior, I wish someone would explain the "logic". N.O.R. must develop a health care package that leaves no one out and affordable. Come on people unite. If there ever was a cause, it's wise to recognize it now—a Retailer's National Health Care Program.

Issues as usual National Health Care, Social Security, Economy, Energy, Defense and all the other issues where nothing gets done have all been brought to the forefront by the candidates in the 2008 election. Won't they ever learn? Better yet, won't the voters ever see through the issues, and the way the manipulation for votes is conducted every four years?

Three of the top Senators two Democrats and one Republican in Congress that ran for President in 2008 hadn't done anything in the past to alleviate the problems. Is there any reason to think they would do anything as President?

Remedy + Repetition = Reward

CHAPTER 15

FREE ENTERPRISE SYSTEM

After a phone conversation with the attorney general's office in Ohio, and having spoken with a couple of staffers in anti-trust law concerning the free enterprise system, it became evident why many people do not vote.

The years it would take in litigation to implement and correct an obstruction of justice is not worth the bother. Monopolies are located just blocks from the state attorney general's office. According to this office, a person must file a complaint for a monopoly to be investigated and broken up. The entrepreneur becomes the scapegoat.

Before any allegations are presented, it is possible that the defense has a cover-up for any wrongdoing. The guilty has ample time to construct a strong deposition. Under the present circumstances, it would be difficult for any judge to find distributors guilty of a price gouging conspiracy and to restrain what they can do to small businesses.

Financial assistance by the bureaucracy is not available for firms that want to locate in a monopolized territory. The government could break up monopolies by supporting financially new wholesale companies, but they will not. Our judicial system as well as the legislative branch does not favor small business regardless of what might be said. Again, retailers are in the lurch.

For many years I was forced to purchase certain items from a single supplier, thus being charged extra. Monopolies must be avoided. Now that we are in the 21st century, owners of small businesses must help to unravel any monopoly as expeditiously as water turns to ice in a freezer.

The time for meaningless chatter is over! It is more advantageous to seek innovation instead of litigation; we will profit from it.

One cannot help but wonder who the silent stockholders of monopolies are. A National Organization of Retailers, with the proper legal support, will be able to destroy in record time, any conspiracy to restrain the success of retailers. With that, the case would be closed. The judicial system needs a jump start.

It is difficult to comprehend this situation if one has not suffered from the effects of monopoly power. A N.O.R. could handle small business legalities involving anti-trust laws.

A computerized system set up by the National Organization of Retailers would indicate immediately the presence of a monopoly in an industrialized nation. When thousands of businesses are buying from the same distributor with no other distributors in sight, the N.O.R would immediately investigate. No private businessperson would be singled out or blamed.

So business does not become motionless, it must activate immediate legal action whenever and wherever necessary. In approaching success in this new millennium, entrepreneurs, with their honesty and integrity, will stabilize the business sector of the economy. Forces of destruction will be eliminated. A new discovery process activated by a National Organization of Retailers will generate a glow of new existence for future entrepreneurs.

Free enterprise will be alive in its true perspective ensuring justice for all. The anti-trust law will be administrated without monopoly-scapegoat recourse. If we honored the Robinson-Pitman anti-trust laws which apply to price discrimination, it would permit N.O.R. to advocate fair pricing. Why have laws if there is no one to enforce honor? Why do government agencies waste taxpayer's money? Yes, we have our work cut out for us.

Let us forget about the wrong doings of others toward small business, and correct the present situation by real workable remedies. The N.O.R. must develop before we lose too many more businesses. Owners of small shops should not have to fight for price equality with the larger stores. Without equalization in wholesale prices of goods to be sold, the owners of small businesses are in danger.

Small business is an occupation where people sometimes lose pay with no bureaucracy support in sight. Whose fault is it? The fault is within small business for having not organized and letting government ruin its very texture. It is an old case of starve the poor while nurturing the rich. It stands to reason why the rich do not reciprocate. Would you ruin a good thing that was going your way? I think not.

Governmental support of any dimension is neglected when it comes to owners of small business in the private sector; thus, entrepreneurs are unjustifiable oppressed.

Remedy + Repetition = Reward

CHAPTER 16

GENERAL STRUCTURES

Station I
Business owners have been in menopause for decades.

There will be a listing of wholesalers, distributors and manufacturers across the nation. This list would include the:

- Company Name
- Address
- Phone Number
- Products
  - types
  - styles
  - prices
- Credit Terms

There will also be a global listing for those who want to purchase from countries outside of the United States.

In the future a retailer will only have to call the organization's 1-800 number to acquire information contained in the computer. Resources will be available to everyone. Merchants would not have to search for information when seeking out new companies to purchase goods for resale. With a listing of companies, the entrepreneurs could choose a company that best suits their needs. The time saved would be phenomenal.

The retailer will have quick, easy access to wholesalers, distributors and manufacturers via the l-800 numbers, the Internet and information requested over the phone. The information would be a free service from the N.O.R. There will be the option of the Internet via computers. Those who have their own computers and printer have the option to use the Internet and printout whatever they need.

Station II

Each small business in any town could be supported by a maintenance, entrepreneurial team made up of electricians, plumbers, carpenters, roofers etc. These business people would be readily available to make repairs. This operation would function much like the emergency car service AAA offers its car members.

However, the difference would be that the merchant whose shop is being repaired would pay a flat fee directly to the maintenance person for services rendered. Entrepreneurs in maintenance who belong to the N.O.R. would be guaranteed business on a permanent basis from N.O.R. shopkeepers; thus, eliminating hassles and cut costs for both parties. "That's what friends are for", beautifully sung by Dionne Warwick, is most apropos. The association would work with maintenance crews to establish guidelines determining the costs.

A maintenance company that I deal with will come the day I call, and send two people. They look around, and then say they will be back the next day. Their excuse is that they have to go back and get the necessary equipment to make repairs.

The business ends up being charged labor time for two, even though they won't begin working until the next day. The N.O.R. maintenance crews will be honest, hard-working people who will get the job done when they come in, and at a reasonable rate.

Today's individual maintenances are too costly for shopkeepers. When retailers operate as an individual the maintenance people can charge costly fees and sometimes the work isn't satisfactory. Where there are no guidelines, greed will innumerably take over capitalism. In professional retail and customer relationships it is important that customer satisfaction is always met in order for the business to operate successfully.

Station III

Franchise business: If a National Organization of Retailers doesn't materialize, the business landscape will remain in a flood zone with one tidal wave after another. The consideration of a franchise business is another option for entrepreneurs. The magazine Small Business Opportunities publishes an annual magazine entitled Franchise 1,000.

According to the publication, franchising is a safe business venture for new entrepreneurs to achieve success. A category listing of franchise businesses contains the company name, address, phone number, a description of the business, establishment information and cost data. Imaginary pictures of the building's design and décor become focused. The graphics, especially in fast food restaurants such as Subway, Rax, Wendy's and White Castle, to name a few, are well known to the public eye.

Its exterior immediately recognizes each restaurant. In the magazine the franchisers are listed:

- Company name
- Address
- Phone number and fax (check computer for up to date)
- Description
- Background
- Hopeful experience
- Training and support
- Cost data

Communications

Grouping together would relieve a lot of the frustration that we face individually. Businesspeople can relate to Shakespeare's line in the soliloquy, "to be or not to be," in the play "Hamlet". Our answer is "to be" with a N.O.R. and "not to be" alone any longer. Shakespeare's famous soliloquy dealt with revenge. Entrepreneurs are dealing with making a difference and providing a better, more prosperous middle class life. Business owners have been in menopause for decades. The business unification transition would be extremely helpful in creating the serenity that was once taken for granted.

An association will make a difference by allowing everyone to be heard. The nation's business community needs to be glued together. The necessary unification will give retailers strength in numbers, a voice in the political arena and ample space to grow.

In the beginning, small business could act alone and survive. It was the American dream. That has all changed due to the overload of bookwork, taxes, reducing the time spent on creative productivity, hazardous government intervention, mega-stores and the outrageous business expenses. Spiders have put together a web that only an organizational group could untangle. N.O.R. will be the component to push business forward, untangling the debris that has stifled us; consequently, boundaries will become unlimited to future prominent retail owners.

Authority

Entrepreneurs need a strong voice of authority. The solution: Ideas, rules and regulation set up by the N.O.R. will be used as guidelines for other members. This is our lifetime destination. If entrepreneurs can eliminate the overload of obstacles, it would be the start of an immediate solution.

Today's standards are vital for the immediate progression of small business. Merchants are always on the defensive side. At present there is no offense for the owner of small business. Let's examine this further. In 1994 the Bureau of Workers Compensation incorrectly put an $8,000 dollar lien on my property through the Attorney General's Office. It was harassment. The Attorney General's Office was informed they had wrongfully and negligently committed an unlawful act. They knew it was NOT the Law. As it turned out the Bureau owed me $366 dollars.

Eight years later, I received a letter from the Attorney General's Office dated 06-22-02.

Dear Sir or Madam:
Enclosed please find the original Release and Satisfaction of Judgment for the above claim. This release pertains to the Judgment we obtained under Ohio Law related to your lien.

Bureau of Workers' Compensation claim: This lien was obtained pursuant to the Ohio Revised Code.

This release must be taken to the Office of the Clerk of the Common Pleas Court in the county indicated for recordation in order that your record be cleared with the court. At that time, you will need to pay whatever filing fee and court costs that may be involved. If you fail to take this release to the Clerk of courts, the lien against your real estate and personal property will not be discharged. It is recommended that you do this immediately.

Supervisor of Accounts Receivable.

Give me a break. Nowhere in the Ohio Revised Code does it say you can wrongfully and knowingly put a lien on anyone. **Obviously, the Attorney General's office didn't read or understand the full context of the Ohio Revised Code.**

Judgment Date: 11-17-94. When clearing the lien, I was told the lien had built up to $11,000 dollars. After receiving the notification of the lien in 1994, one follow up notice and talking to the Attorney General Office, it was assumed the lien had been cleared.

Where is my assessment for something done vindictively? **It's the law, wouldn't you think! No, it doesn't work that way**. There is no recourse for the owner of small business. If there were, then there would be a radiant light at the end of the merchant's dilemma. Ethics is nonexistent in many laws. How sad is that?

The essence of equal standards is for the local, state and federal governmental departments to follow the same rules as those that are followed by shop owners. Then one can say—"It's the Law." No way was justice served in this case.

Let's Move on. Ideals cannot be won if standards are not met. Americans are paying a higher price for items each year. While making the rich richer, and the poor poorer, the noble middle class remains idle forcing some into poverty. Nothing will intensify the N.O.R. more than the development of a, with lobbyists, business structures, support systems and training programs for entrepreneurs. Then, and only then our dreams and ideals will materialize.

Small business must stop being abused and see that employers are compensated.

Station IV

Legislative Branch

Again, we have another—legislative branch—that is a problem for merchants. Why? They refuse to do the job for which they were elected without causing problems for others. The grape-vine laws governing small business have root-rot.

Technology advancements are flying faster than the speed of light. This is the speed by which owners of small business must proceed.

Base structures are essential for members of small business to gain protection equivalent with all other occupations. Peace and security will emerge. The structures that are important have been designed, but it's up to all the members of the N.O.R. to agree and fulfill the commitment.

The Case

Epilogue

There are a lot of facts, hypotheses, some generalizations and a few personal thoughts, but NOTHING compares to the experience—the ups and downs, the sleepless nights, surviving through every obstacle and most of all maintaining equilibrium. The American Dream is in shambles.

I have learned the fact that it is a dog eat dog world, ethics are passé and seldom does the lion physically appear for the cubs. Anyone in small business is forced (paying taxes without representation) to support some very bad elements, and would like to see good prevail. What little is preserved of ethics, morals and faith are present because of public scrutiny and the consciousness of the people themselves. Education is our future.

N.O.R. will unite to create an updated version of the real American Dream. The Dream needs to be brightened to the level it once was. The ideas of spirituality, morals, ethics, family and unconditional love were the primary standards when the dream thrived in America.

Business leaders can no longer be content with present business practices. We must be concerned for the survival of small business by transformations in society—socially, economically and with political structures. We must restore principles that are livable both business and family wise. We must elevate ourselves to the standards that govern all other professions in society.

As mega-stores are monopolizing the cities, small businesses have seen sweet wine turn into sour grapes. Without any kind of assistance from the federal government such as grants, low interest loans or any other means to compete with giant stores, individual entrepreneurs have been forced to lower incomes and in some cases the loss of their businesses.

To add insult to injury, universities are taking the taxpayer's money in addition to tax exemptions, and going into direct competition with private enterprise. Is there no salvation? Yes, there is a savior, the N.O.R. that can restore great faith in the forgotten millions of owners of small businesses across America. My prayer is to see businesspeople stand by their stores until an association is formed, and protect Newton's law of gravity with centrifugal force blocking any further damage to the utopian dream.

The American Dream will be again saturated with honesty, integrity, compassion, faith, understanding and ethics without selfish materialistic influence, and filled with an over abundance of family love and friends, replacing greed or super capitalism and conducting ourselves in a professional manner. With a National Organization of Retailers based on the fine upstanding individuals enduring hard work, honesty and ethics—small business will reach stratospheric levels.

Remedy + Repetition = Reward.

CHAPTER 17

ADMINISTRATION

What a better way to build an administration than restoring the words of Abraham Lincoln ". . . that the nation under God shall have a new birth of freedom, and that government of the people, by the people and for the people shall not perish from the earth."

These immortal words live forever. To reverse the devastation confronting employers is the ultimate purpose of unification. The framers of the N.O.R. will have to become familiar with all areas of business in order to serve all its members' needs. Although business people basically have similar problems, some will also face different obstacles than others. However, N.O.R.'s ample membership will be heavy support for leaders in guiding retailers where they need to go to accomplish their goals.

Coming together provides us with the solutions to compete with corporate America. Constructive ideas established by our forefathers such as President Thomas Jefferson, President John F. Kennedy and Benjamin Franklin along with President Lincoln will gain momentum enriching the American Dream.

Congress allocates finances to many areas with the taxpayers' money, but allows nothing for independent business people. Alone, quality is a lost virtue. Together, a 's leaders can lobby for equal treatment that is long overdue.

As a unified group, the association can cast their block vote, per se, for government leaders who support private enterprise. The elected officials of the N.O.R will not tolerate satisfying greed and temptation.

It is this exact sort of leadership that led to the demise of such large corporations as Enron, World Com and others, which have fallen under investigation. The only way to constructively advance a capitalistic economy is by following ethical standards in leadership.

Sharing in corrupt means by bribing Congress is simply not the retailer's perception of correct action, either. Too many government impurities have surfaced. If politicians want to prostitute themselves, entrepreneurs will not meet their means. The conspirators of corruption that weigh heavily on the two-party system, just as it does big corporation has vanished voters belief in political integrity. Voters have expressed their dissatisfaction in candidates by staying home on Election Day.

Voter dissatisfaction can be easily corrected. Instead of present politicians telling people what they are going to do, they should inform us of their past accomplishments. If there is evidence of passing legislation that favors the entrepreneurs of the nation, then non-voting business people may consider going back to the polls. However, a spoken promise without commitment only enlarges the numbers that stay away.

Another stronger option to consider is a third party. Republicans are far to the right and Democrats further to the left, which leaves the center open. The state of Minnesota proved this theory correct by electing a third party candidate—Gov. Jesse Ventura. Within six months of his administration, Gov. Ventura had given back money in high numbers to the state's taxpaying citizens.

A third party that exemplifies honesty, ethics and integrity could easily satisfy the National Organization of Retailers. Overpowering words of wisdom followed by accomplishment is praiseworthy in the world's new economy. Stepping on anyone to achieve our goals will not be tolerated. We don't need some dork CEO, CFO and other executives taking advantage of others.

There are some highly skilled CEOs, CFOs and executives deserving of millions of dollars for they have produced billions for their companies and have done it well.

Mega-stores will no longer be a threat. Price discrimination will no longer exist. There is room for all to achieve success if the playing field is level.

With every component in place, the emphasis will be to elevate all the business owners with less focus on buildings or materialistic achievements. Business should not take priority over family. NOR will take a back seat to the business landscape. Working as one unit makes family success achievable.

The N.O.R. leaders will generate wholesome and clean leadership. As the development of the association progresses, improvements will materialize for a more substantial administrative structure. All members will come together for the vital purpose of producing a N.O.R. type government that is of the people, by the people, for the people and excludes no one—all is the people.

Chapter 18

N.O.R.

Setting up a National Organization of Retailers requires an extensive study of associations that are now in operation. Shop owners must eliminate being ignored, harassed and unnecessarily abused. This has been covered up for too long. Toleration of negative feedback is no longer acceptable. It's no secret as to the accomplishments of people acting together. An association is a big step toward achieving equality.

In October of 1997, the Senate Finance Committee held three days of hearings on the abusiveness enacted by the Internal Revenue Service toward the taxpayers, many of whom were in business. The Senate Finance Committee, after the hearings, decided to reform the Internal Revenue Service. Right! Again, they will try to cover their last blunder by creating another one.

This same abusiveness exists in the way government harasses other small businesses. It is not crystal clear as to where this type of abnormal behavior toward small shops developed or how it reached such monumental proportions. However, one thing is transparent. The Senate sits with one finger up their noses and in unison they all say, Duh! Supposedly, these are educated people, but they don't seem to know what is going on in the private sector.

Every caution must be taken to ensure that the leaders of the N.O.R. keep themselves briefed on all business activities. If one individual is mistreated, we want reparations. People are needed ethically, logically and spiritually to make the right decisions on all issues. Computer technology must be the pace at which the N.O.R. aspires. No one shall be overlooked.

Regardless of how much money is turned over to the government by small business, there is no political clout or financial support for hard work. It is apparent that we receive nothing for our efforts. Keeping individual and group needs in perspective, the unification will represent the long-term goal.

One proposal would be to follow the procedure set up by any state's education association, such as the Ohio Education Association (O.E.A). Each state that starts its own association must organize local units, progressing forward to a National Organization for Retailers. This will produce a more unified and tightly knit association of merchants with only one main purpose: to gain respect and support so small business can survive in the 21st century.

It was once said, "Never have so many, had so little, for so long." This is a trite and common cliché that is true. Now begins the long struggle of the group that has been repressed. As computers have reshaped the economical future of our great land, most retailers conceptualize a higher focus on enterprise. Lobbyists are needed in Washington, D.C. to change the business landscape in government.

In the future, once new legislation is in progress, N.O.R. will be the equalizing force that gives balance to our system. Both parties, the government and small businesses, will agree and be equally satisfied.

The following is a proposal for the foundations of offices. Four national locations are suggested for offices to be built on land outside the cities listed. Sites mentioned are optional—some other areas may be more acceptable.

City
- Pittsburgh, Pennsylvania (northeastern)
- Atlanta, Georgia (southeastern)
- Albuquerque, New Mexico (southwestern)
- Lake Tahoe, Nevada (northwestern)

A building will be constructed for the national offices of association executives and their staffs with an auditorium, cafeteria, lounge and pharmacy for starters.

Areas will be designated for the future sites of motels, shopping malls, recreation centers, gym, fitness center, entertainment, restaurants and movies suitable for the whole family. A place of worship is another element for the N.O.R. members and their children. The buildings surrounding the executive office can create a household and vocational atmosphere.

The family oriented environment will be the first step in returning to the real values of togetherness. Family values are problematic these days, so it is time to do something to stimulate ways to create a family setting.

By facing every problem head on, the necessary criteria for better surroundings will emerge for the present and future generations. Business owners taking command in the leadership of a progressive movement for family life will be in tune with the phenomenal twenty-first century.

Honor and Respect

An economy taking two wage earners to support a family, pay for a house and buy a car, is not a good representation of family values. One parent is needed at home with the children until each child has reached maturity. Chances of this are unlikely until the costs of products are lowered.

Higher prices and higher wages make for more tax money, less buying power, and a decrease in employment. Is it necessity for both parents to work? However, the country is in immediate danger. If Congress has their way, it will not only take the parents but the children working at an early age to cover the needed expenses at home.

The constructive way to get society back on track is to downsize economics. Proprietorship economics within a N.O.R. can achieve a valuable ingredient that is very much necessary for the impoverished people.

According to an article in Fortune magazine, all family time is quality time. Family love is full time responsibility. Parents should be present even if they are not needed. There is nothing better than children and parents being together on a permanent basis.

My father never missed a meal with his seven children—he was the personification of family values. My Dad could never be replaced by any group of people, such as a nanny or day care service. His family overload was managed permitting each child the best of family life. Loving every minute of being at the center of the perimeter, my father sent his children beyond the perimeter while he remained the solid foundation. The children in turn became the main structure allowing their children to extend the perimeter.

The unification of the entrepreneur's family and business lives will stabilize the community and keep the American Dream alive. The objective of the four national office locations is to perform business as well as make every effort to keep the family together. The businessperson from near and not so far away can go to the executive meetings and programs while their relatives are nearby. There will be a place for all family members whose business owner is attending conferences for whatever reason. Life will take on new meaning by getting back to the basics—the real family structure.

The people of small business can build a vigorous trust in community life through ethics, hard work and honesty. At present we are lacking the balance of a good family life to correspond with a good business life. N.O.R. is the solution to all these problems. Unification will provide a healthier and happier family, provided that materialistic achievements do not stand in the way.

Raising children is what life is all about. Time away from the children is precious moments that can never be replaced. Life is fragile. Daily love will produce no regrets later in life. Your children are important— don't leave home without them. The greatest enjoyment of life, the time spent with offspring, is priceless. Personal parental guidance and love must be given on a daily basis until all of the children are mature. Children are not like animals and shouldn't be treated as such. Most children are incapable of raising themselves. The hypothesis is that the less time parents spend with their children, the less time the children are going to spend with mom and dad in their old age.

Materialistic worship is stunting the development of a brighter and better parent-child relationship. "Cat on a Hot Tin Roof," by William Faulkner, illustrates the contrasts of relationships between two brothers with their father. One brother starves for the father's affection, both physically and mentally. The other brother is only interested in inheriting his parent's materialistic possessions. The question is: who has the better life? Let's not kid ourselves. We all know the answer to that question.

Again, it is compassion, understanding and basic humanity that will lead us through societies' challenges in this new millennium. Setting up a N.O.R. with a labor allows us to leap instead of limp through the twenty-first century.

Eleanor Roosevelt said the following in 1927:

> "The big question before our people today is whether we are to be more material in our thinking, judging administrative success by economic results entirely and leaving out all other achievements. History shows that a nation interested primarily in material things invariably is on a downward path. Great wealth has ruined every nation since the day that Cheops laid the corner stone of the Great Pyramid, not because of any inherent wrong in wealth, but because it became the ideal and the idol of the people. Phoenicia, Carthage, Greece, Rome, Spain, all bear witness to this truth".

Although the remark was made in 1927, it's no surprise it holds true today. Quoting from the Oxford dictionary greed means "excessive desire". Ten years ago Iraq and more recently greed obliterated Egypt and Libya.

Some CEOs have turned their successes into failures by being extremely greedy. Now, they find themselves behind bars washing dishes. Their multimillion dollar paychecks were not enough. Anyone who mentions that greed is good does not have their priorities straight. It's one of the seven deadly sins.

My hope and pray is that the children who will be leading this great nation in the future will not emulate liars, thieves, cheaters, low moral standards and representatives of greed. Businesspeople must keep their financial life in true perspective by advocating capitalism not super capitalism meaning greed. Although a dream is just that a dream, there should be enough room for those that can pursue their real American dream in an honorable fashion personifying capitalism. If greed interferes then all is lost. According to first lady Eleanor

Roosevelt great wealth will ruin any nation when it becomes the ideal and the idol of the people. Ethics ensures the longevity of a stable democracy. An entrepreneurial association will succeed in putting the country back on the <u>right track</u>. Our present leaders have ignored or eradicated the constitutional values of our forefathers that made this country great. Procrastination is giving us limited time on something that should have happened a long time ago.

It's sad but do you know one of the main ways to get the support we need from politicians? **All donations by owners of small business are given to the politician or politicians that can best fulfill their needs.**

Republicans might be able to dismantle s and collective bargaining from workers, such as teachers, nurses, firefighters, and all workers' groups who basically contribute to Democrats. There is no way they can interfere with our contributions. Small business will gain the honor and respect deserved.

GRAPH—OUTLINE

National

President
Secretary & Staff

Vice–President
Secretary & Staff

Secretary
Secretary & Staff

Treasurer
Secretary & Staff

1.	2	3	4	5
Director	Director	Director	Director	Director
Sec. & Staff	Sec. & Staff	Sec. & Staff	Sec. & Staff	Sec. & Staff
Chairman of membership and organizational development	Chairman of direct assistance personnel	Chairman of legal services Tax Structure	Chairman of operations Training members Fed, State, & Local field assistance	Chairman of seminars and programs Printed material and business computer technology

6	7	8	9	10
Director	Director	Director	Director	Director
Sec. & Staff	Sec. & Staff	Sec. & Staff	Sec. & Staff	Sec. & Staff
Computer and Programmer Info. Analysis Projection of New Ideas	Retirement Health and General Insurance	Financial and College Assistance	Promotions Purchasing and Merchandising Price Control	Labor Union Lobbyists Political Strategy

State

President
Secretary & Staff

Vice—President
Secretary & Staff

Secretary
Secretary & Staff

Treasurer
Secretary & Staff

All five directors will work to advise and educate locals on all issues.

Director
Secretary & Staff

Director
Secretary & Staff

Director
Secretary & Staff

State Seminars	Legal Assistance	Human Relations
Programs	Tax Assistance	Retirement
Direct Assistance	Government Assistance	Health
Disaster Relief	Minimum Wage (Employers)	College Program

Director	Director	State Building
Secretary & Staff	Labor Union Secretary & Staff	Administrator & Staff

Computer	Labor Relations	Maintenance
Operations	Lobbyists	Cafeteria
Membership	Grievances	
Dues		
Family Excellence		

Planning Executives
Secretaries & Staffs

Manager of Maintenance	Manager of Mall
Secretary & Staff	Secretary & Staff
For and within national building	Managers /or Owners for each new
Building Upkeep	complex as it is developed
Daily Maintenance	

Manager of Motel
Secretary & Staff

Taking a lot of time to formulate all the structures and landscape, the outlook for various positions will be established as needed. A long, drawn out procedure taking a great deal of planning, building and engineering must be supervised with plenty of foresight. Cleverly skilled and crafted individuals using ethics and logical methods of knowledge and experience are needed to handle the job. The focus is the long-term goal.

Facilitating a resort/city atmosphere with everything centrally located leaves little traveling from one place to another. Recreation, events, shopping, banking needs, restaurants and ventures of all kinds are available. While conferences are being held, the family can take in the attractive sites; thus, the plans for a pleasurable design must be well surveyed.

After plans are acceptable, then construction can start.

CHAPTER 20

NATIONAL ORGANIZATION OF RETAILERS

Purpose
The purpose of building a National Organization of Retailers is to develop a supportive force vigorous enough to accomplish the real American Dream for all owners of small business. This will allow small businesses to progress at a faster pace and be more competitive with large corporations.

The organization will be built on honesty, ethics, integrity, compassion and understanding without corruption. N.O.R. will also be gigantic in proportion. There will be no blinders to our aspirations of a genuine future for the family, rewards for honest workers, benefits for America's deserving and preserving the American Dream.

Congress
N.O.R. will be able to send lobbyists to Washington, D.C. for fair representation of all owners of small business. The association can put a stop to negative legislation that is destroying the many small shops. Mutual respect and support for all of our grievances will be addressed and answered. A big achievement would be to persuade Congress to share the pot with owners of small business when they allocate the tax money for education, technology, defense and government.

Proprietorship Economics
Merchants need an organization that provides solutions to problems instead of solutions "per se" that create more problems. A

unit capable of answering and eradicating all problems while presenting all grievances within our political structure would be helpful. An association can financially assist small businesses with emphasis on solving the difficulty.

We will still send lobbyists to Washington, D.C. to persuade elected officials to support the cause of small business throughout the United States; however, due to the fact that they respond in a lackadaisical manner in passing legislation we cannot foresee any immediate developments. A more realistic view will need to be adopted. We must concentrate and find the solution that best serves us without expecting any outside help or interference. The operation must keep everyone and everything in authentic perspective.

Family

A priority would be to bring the family unit back to family ideals, through the unconditional parenthood of love and trust. N.O.R. would be a helpful unit to take the main interest away from the materialistic and social atmospheric false ideas. An environment for the whole family at the four national organizations would be ideal. A parent in each family proudly saying, "I am a dedicated and happy homemaker" is what I hope and pray for. That has to be one of the most beautiful lines ever spoken.

Security

A goal would be to develop a secure foundation that would stabilize all owners of small businesses and their families in the twenty-first century.

Constitution

Preamble:

We the retailers of America will unite for the betterment of mutual understanding and agreeable compromises between the government and business owners by creating a vigorous trust through a relationship of honesty, integrity, compassion and understanding. There will be equal treatment for all of the members of the N.O.R. By shaping a new American entrepreneurial landscape that rewards the hard working community of business people, N.O.R.'s Proprietorship Economics shall both satisfy it's members and clientele. We, as a group, will honor and respect the solutions set up by the leaders of a National Organization of Retailers to better serve the American people. Equality and justice is the essence. We will change the business landscape by rewarding the many benefits to retailers that government workers receive.

Our motto will be:
Remedy + Repetition = Reward

Objectives

To elevate small business to the same level as other professions in American society.

To see that each member is treated fairly with the pay and benefits that is equal to other professions.

Reward hard working and honest people of this earth.

Unite for economic, political and survivor reasons.

United we will succeed by an active voice that will be heard. Communication is the central theme, but hard work is the only answer; therefore, deeds must follow ethical words to achieve our goal.

Organization

Officers: President, Vice President, Secretary and Treasurer will be selected and elected to form an administrative structure that will satisfy the members of a N.O.R. at each of the four national areas. An executive director will chair each department of importance having one's own staff.

The selection of Lobbyists will provide answers in Washington. These people will operate like the TV quiz show Jeopardy. The lobbyists will provide the answers allowing Congress to issue the questions. This should allow business owners to get to where they need to go. Look at it now. It seems the only rest for entrepreneurs is when Congress is in recess. Our legislators directly advocate very little if anything for all owners of small business. However, there is a different scenario for big corporations. Wonder why?

The association of a N.O.R. will require an extensive study. Once the main format is set up, the authoritative completion of the necessary chain of command will fall into place. All information will be followed up by the four presidents, to their staffs, executive committees and to each individual owner of small business through the Internet and newsletters.

Membership

Any individual who has operated a small business successfully for over one year will be invited to join. All entitlements will belong to each and every member of the association.

The officers will all work for a set salary. There will be no freebies, no expense account and no free travel. All luxuries will be provided at the N.O.R. sites. Each officer must have at least five years experience of running a business. The prerequisite will be determined as to the financial condition of their respective businesses. Again, it must be remembered these are proposals; therefore, other ideas may be more acceptable.

Each officer at the national and state levels will receive an office with all of the necessary equipment to function properly. The President shall be in office no more than two years so as not to monopolize the power of such an organization. Annual pay will be $200,000 per year and $100,000 severance pay, adjusted as needed. One has the option of remaining on the staff as an advisor.

However, any pay increase, perks or bonuses may not be in play. Many companies, corporations and other business industries have suffered greatly due to the fact executives drained the financial resources with outlandish luxuries.

The business composite is one of merit and equality to members as well as officers. N.O.R leaders will be the providers of honesty, integrity, compassion and understanding. Deeds will follow without hesitation the communications that our leaders establish.

Leaders of the N.O.R. will balance body and mind for the good of all. The association will not be concerned about materialistic remnants of society. Its concern is family and loved ones.

Small-business owners' most difficult job will be to elect leaders who are lovers of mankind and not ego worn. Ethics has also lost its place in society and must be reestablished by the business community. Ethics shall be the essence of the officer's protocol—spoken, applied and idolized.

Ayn Rand, author of "The Fountainhead", "Atlas Shrugged" and other best sellers, once said "upper classes are a nation's past; the middle class is its future." Right. In order to achieve harmony and balance, class distinction must not invade the scope of entrepreneurs. A more structured authoritative environment, with fairness for all the officers and members of N.O.R. will protect and enlighten the future of the middle class.

Committees

All the necessary committees will set up after the officers of N.O.R. are established. Once the state organizations are formed, then local business owners can come together and arrange their own officers and committees.

Annual Dues

The annual dues will be set according to the state convention's decision. Dues are to be kept at a minimum. After dues are established for the state and national organizations, then officers in turn can allocate the amount of cash per structural division.

Expenses

Money is the bloodline of the association. For every national, state and local level, integrity will be its guide. Any financial misleading will be cause for dismissal. When it comes to money, we've all had untrustworthy employees and know the suffering they have caused. Thirty-five thousand businesses went bankrupt one year because of employee thievery, and many others suffered severely; therefore, business survivors know the value of honesty within themselves and those we supervise.

Laws

Arrangement laws will prevail:

Article I:

I-a.—Governing: President, Vice President, Secretary, Treasurer, and staffs—executive directors and staffs—the deciding powers will be the levels. The members will select leaders at the national, state and local levels. The locals will select representatives to attend state meetings twice a year.

I-b.—A more simplified version of Roberts' "Rules of Order", the book about parliamentary procedure, is the essence in conducting meetings. No meetings will display dinners unless the family is involved. Duties and responsibilities will be handled efficiently. This organization will act upon the problems with one solution after another. Unnecessary litigation will be eliminated. If old business is not solved, then stressing remedies on the agenda will be a meeting's importance. Positive answers will make for effective communications. We'll strive for innovation.

Article II:—Legislative Procedure:

Committees: The leaders of N.O.R will establish meetings, duties and responsibilities. The first order of business is to develop a circuit to reach all, or as many as possible, retailers across the country. Would they be interested in joining a retailer's association? A standardized form of acknowledgement is recommended. Once the numbers are actively recorded, then the development of an association will be approachable. The Internet would speed up the project.

Lobbying: Members will have to decide what is needed from Congress and work toward the long-term ideals of the N.O.R. Lobbyists will meet with members of Congress to express the grievances and goals. Any encouragement would be helpful to the cause. A labor is absolutely necessary.

Article III—Dues: to be set up by each state's executive committee

Article IV—Guidelines to follow for national, state and local regions

Article V—Commitment: (1) by officers to further enhance the construction of the N.O.R., S.O.R. and L.O.R., by building the associations with the retailers of small business. Goal: 100% membership. (2) To dedicate oneself for the advancement of all entrepreneurs across the nation. (3) To satisfy the needs, interests and concerns of all owners of small businesses. (4) To assure that integrity, honesty, compassion and understanding are the keys to success. (5) To assure that all governing done with ethics, logic, morals and not *mala fides*. (6) To simplify the "Rules of Order" so meetings go smoother and faster.

VI—Computers: (1) To keep data, record all memberships, facts and information on small business, explanation of each association— N.O.R., S.O.R., and L.O.R.—and how the set-up works. 2) Explanation of all the different structures and their importance. (3) All legislation that surrounds the lobbyists. (4) All up to date information of small business recorded on the Internet.

VII—Family: All associations working within the means of a full workday without the interference of family life. Once property is developed and headquarters have been arranged, then the property development of a national mall will be projected for all family activities. The four sites will house national headquarters, offices, apartments, motels, restaurants, shopping centers, theater, movie rentals, spas or fitness centers, recreation area, casinos, bars, golf course, tennis, racquetball and basketball courts, free and ample parking, churches and/or cathedrals, doctors, lawyers, and other professionals, medical buildings with pharmacies, automotive service stations and any other service providing a supreme family atmosphere.

We want to make our organization a unique and interesting endeavor, and an organization that exemplifies ethics and hard work. Capitalism can become a greedy hard-nosed piece of machinery that ignores the happiness life has to offer. The N.O.R. will alleviate many of, if not all, the problems small businesses are subjected to.

Remedy + Repetition = Reward

The National Education Association is the greatest protective institution that was ever built. Small business must follow. It is ridiculous that groups of people have to join an association to get where they need to go, but even more ABSURED NOT TO UNITE.

The Ohio Education Association started in 1851 and it wasn't until 75 years later that they started making waves. The main tidal wave was in the 1970's that the real progress was achieved. Many school strikes occurred. Once all school strikes were settled, the schoolteachers of the future were on an ocean liner that moves full speed ahead and hasn't lost one iota of motion. My observation is that their has far surpassed the teamster's. No has a more concrete structure consisting of leader's with integrity, ethics and morals that has mesmerized the teaching profession and gained the full support of all the teachers that belong to the O.E.A.

The Ohio Teacher's Association was developed and engineered by six men, four in their twenties and two in their thirties. It's a shame they didn't live to see the remarkable progress. Even today, their association leaders have to go the full cycle of labor relations to achieve continuous success. Not only are their pay and benefits accelerating, but also these leaders have a retirement system that's worth studying. History has proven that an association is the only way to go.

Is it ironic that Congress doesn't need a? They supply themselves, but only intimidate people in other fields by spending the tax money for luxuries unknown to hard workers. The time is now for the owners of small business to organize and get their full share of the pot. The best way to do that is for small business to unite and develop methods like the National, State and local Education Associations. The foundation of associations have already been paved and proven by most occupations; therefore, our uniting will escalate to economic proportions in no time. Given the full cooperation of all retailers across the nation the N.O.R. will be successful.

Once succeeding the N.O.R. will be able to fulfill its' own destination. We no longer will rely on Congress, where many of our problems originated, to answer our grievances or needs. We will establish our own form of community through unifying. Congress in turn will have to move mountains to gain our block of votes. Positive results in the big picture for retailers may require electing all new representation of Senators and Representatives in Congress whose familiarity will breed content.

Our endurance is astronomical. After many elections and voting for people who have broken their promises, the 1987 election being, "read my lips, no new taxes," and in 1991 a universal health care package didn't materialize and the lies in the 21st Century has vanished all creditability of America's leaders. The trust is gone.

It should be evident by now that the N.O.R. is the only way to get where owners of small businesses needed to be years ago. Our leaders will be trustworthy. They are representatives of small business putting forth their best efforts to achieve N.O.R.'s goal. The executives of the N.O.R. will live no better than the businessperson that he/she is representing. Leaders of the N.O.R. will have the same luxuries as the people they serve. Any deviation from the norm will be excruciating. Through modern technology we must begin to accomplish the necessary preparation to be victorious in this millennium.

Times were said to be rich and prosperous, so why are owners of small business so broke the last ten years? Could it be isolating us from one another by not organizing? I think so. Is it because we are defenseless? I presume so. Can it be because there is no political clout? I believe so. There is a multitude of reasons, but one thing is for real— everything is working against the independent retailer. Frustrations cannot continue. The negativity must be minimized and eventually eliminated. We must create an organization and keep the American Dream alive by establishing solutions to all business problems without favoritism

Ex-Governor of Minnesota, Jesse Ventura, said in the August 1999 issue of Home Business Magazine, "The best thing that government can do is to get out of the way of the private sector, and let entrepreneurship bloom." To flourish we must discover an affirmative agenda to interact with government or prosper without.

An unexpected insult to owners of small business, who have managed their businesses honorably, has jeopardized merchant's integrity when government gives mismanagement rewards. If CEOs, CFOs and executives had managed their paychecks, perks and bonuses according to the profit and loss of a corporation, then there would be no reason for a bailout.

How can you justify directly bailing out corporations while small businesses go bankrupt and all jobs are lost. Small business is the backbone of our economy. When the small businesses are losing millions of employers and employees jobs, they should get the same privilege given large corporation to balance the scales of justice.

Talk is cheat. Their justification for bailing out AIG is hogwash. The **GOOD** workers are the ones losing their jobs.

Just another example of government's lost virtues when it comes to America's middle and poor class. Entrepreneurs must unite or the same beat goes on. Power and money are culprits that demonize the creditability of hard working people.

While bad decisions of big corporations are rewarded, good decisions of owners of small businesses go without. Is that the American way? I hope not.

CHAPTER 21

PART I

A Summary of the Retail Environment

Modern technology has brought a new dimension to American public responses to retailers. The illustration of consumer purchasing represents a new retailer commitment that requires more provisions at a higher standard of services.

Challenges must be met with greater manageability, excellent serviceability and eminent compatibility. Employees are required to have a pleasing personality, a positive attitude, enthusiasm and fast service, coupled with a store's excellent pricing, selection of merchandise and goods of superior quality.

Sizeable profits along with a large volume of buyers are necessary in the new economy as well as the old economy of small business. Again, the business landscape must meet the constant changes in order to achieve success. A National Organization of Retailers can relieve the overload so workers can solve contemporary modifications in rapid succession.

A new set of economics in business relations demands more time to constructively acknowledge and fulfill answers to consumer responses. Sufficiently achieving our goals, there is a strong belief we can better the supervisor—clerk—customer relationship by offering better benefits to employees in our industrial workshop.

National Organization of Retailers and Government

Lobbyists selected to represent small business, must construct a force to block any negative legislation that interferes with the energetic workings of the N.O.R. Once united a dynamic force will be an influential powerhouse economically, politically and socially.

Whoever said patience is a virtue never waited for Congress to pass a law of any substance favorable to small business. Political promises to private enterprise have dissolved quicker than the ebb tide that sweeps over the sandy shore before retreating back to the ocean.

N.O.R. can control its own destiny. Ethically solving all business issues N.O.R. will move as swiftly as e-mail in cyberspace.

Inspiration
- Making a positive difference for all retailers in the business landscape.
- Affirmative belief is of real value for hard work and honesty.
- Corruption, disloyalty and dishonesty are nullified without reward.
- Bring eternal life to the American Dream with all the congenial significance it stands for.

Motto
Solutions for new changes will be enforced through proprietorship economics.

Remedy + Repetition = Reward

Goal

To help retailers endure hardships until grievances have been resolved by the administration, and to continue to strive for future goals until they are accomplished.

Code of Ethics
- Treating every member fairly, N.O.R. leaders will:
- Respect the worth and dignity of each entrepreneur
- Reward hard work, loyalty and perseverance
- Value and promote integrity, honesty, compassion, **ethics** and understanding

- Support anyone who is having trouble
- Share a vision of warmth and protection
- Equal treatment, one for all—all for one
- Make every effort to ensure that life is fair

Ethics is the protocol. Due to the fact that powerful leaders have stepped on the toes of small-business owners and let greed and temptation influence their judgment doesn't mean that the loss of right and wrong is justified. Irrational behavior is not acceptable. Once we have turned our lives around and restored our middle class status, then it would be most noble to not turn our back on the less fortunate. Let's put the country back on the right track.

Employee

After many years of business experience and over one-thousand employees I have discovered only two types of employees:

The honest:

Employees who are honest will establish their credibility by fulfilling the following: charisma, sincerity, honesty, integrity, reliability, attitude, responsibility, personality, subordination, appearance and be mature in their approach. An honest employee satisfies the relaxation any employer needs.

The dishonest:

If an employee is dishonest, the animosity weights heavily and everything becomes chaotic. Steps must be taken to see that the employee becomes honest or else replacement is necessary.

PART II

Summary—Delayed but not denied

In small business, the goal is to make enough profit to support the welfare of the business; its employer and employees while satisfying government intervention. In order to make a profit the employer must balance the budget of assets and liabilities. Each self-employed person must continuously be accountable for all creditors (i.e. the I.R.S., banks, utilities, the government or anyone who is anti-small business). Controlling numerous trivialities becomes a burden.

The entrepreneur is defenseless. One has no guaranteed wage, no benefits (including insurance of any kind) and is not given any grievances other associations strive to achieve. Dependence on legislators is a lost cause. With no organization watching over to protect the business, the employer must seek assistance elsewhere.

A manager's job consists of constant repetition of the rules and regulations that are expected and to be honored by all of the employees. Any retailer's competency can only be as good as the adequacy of one's employees. Sacrificing or sharing some of the merchant's potential is necessary to bring out the best capacity of the many workers. The employer's position to the hired help is similar to the workings of a parent-child relationship. The merchant must act as a leader, and guide the employees in all the constructive methods that one (the store owner) has been taught or experienced. He/she must be able to relate skillfully through communications any issue that affects the business. The owner of small business must go without reward, recognition and continuously lean on themselves for support.

The self-employed person must have a complete understanding of human nature and be able to relate to each employee when the time is needed. He/she must be mentally and physically alert and not drained by stress or strain. Surprisingly, one must have the capacity to overlook a paranoid atmosphere; therefore, any prospect of paranoia must be considered self-preservation. In order to maintain self-preservation, the employer must be capable of accepting bad criticism along with good criticism.

Given an ideal situation, the employer will radiate, reflect and generate magnetism and competency. If an employer has the energy and strength, he/she will achieve their goals regardless of the determinants created by adversaries.

Congress creating a minimum wage leaves the merchants incapable of rewarding superior employees. The owner is unable to provide proper wages for his/her employees; therefore, the employer cannot gain the faithful respect of the best workers. A tax reduction would be a more effective supplement to increase wages.

The staggering business sector receives very little help from the government. As according to the criteria, the government controls the bulk of the business profit through taxation. The tax money is then allocated to those in defense, technology, education and big government. The money is also used for welfare, unemployment and food stamps. Small business loses out, regardless. A larger allotment for the already endowed is the current and ongoing trend. Entrepreneurs must remain like any naked Greek statue unmarred by any obstacle.

Question: Why isn't small business rewarded heavily?

Answer: Small business is not organized.

Mr. Cromie's statement rings true, "The more one considers an organization, the less sense it makes not to have one." All I can ask is, "Why?" Why and how have we come this far without a formal organization? Therefore, I hope each of us comes away from this book feeling not only confident, but also motivated.

As it stands, government entities, payroll and other expenses to run the business deplete the entrepreneur's profit. Just in one year all my utilities have increased considerably. Some claim the high cost of oil caused inflation with stagnant economic activity and high unemployment.

Yet, Oil has fallen from around $150 to $38 and then back up to $80 a barrel. Gasoline has come down, but utilities remain the same. Justice didn't prevail. We were lied to. In all reality we can't pass this on to the customer. Wow, if we had a National Organization of Retailers in which all entrepreneurs were members utility companies would be blown out of the ball park.

As I write this manuscript I often wonder how God will judge man's inhumanity toward men especially the liars, thieves and the unfaithful. Utility companies are reducing our profit to enhance their paychecks; thus leaving some families short of food, proper heat and electricity.

Adding to Washington's overspending and a dip in the overall economy, big government and higher taxes does not work for middle class America. It never did! Unity is the deciding factor for retailers that own and manage a small business.

A National Organization of Retailers would supply us with the defense needed to challenge government and mega-stores. The sound philosophy and solid foundation of the N.O.R. will provide a competitive edge especially in ethics, honesty, compassion and understanding to gain control of our future.

Faithful leaders offering a vision of renewed energy and relief for the entrepreneur would do for starters. There would be a vision of serenity and protection for all merchants unlike any change we have ever seen. This change would represent a personal relationship—treat others as you would like to be treated—that is based on a true family-like situation.

The focus is on prayer, family, friends, hard work, honesty, understanding, compassion, relaxation and excellent relationships. Other behaviors to include are conquering all adversity, customer satisfaction, a lot of good luck and above all, integrity and ethics.

All entrepreneurs must continue to ride out the storm on a raft floating in an ocean full of waves until the umbrella of security and protection transpires. Again, the time is now for the formation of the N.O.R.; there are no extensions, no procrastinations, and no time to mope. We are many individuals with many diversifications and now we must conform into one large unit. While we unite our individualism can still be maintained. We must represent and prove that the American Dream is still alive.

To quote bodybuilder and Physique Artist Extraordinaire, Russ Testo, "Keep your dream alive." N.O.R. must personify that American dream.

The Dream is to establish for small-business owners a blanket of security and protection for continued success with rewards, benefits and happiness. This will be achieved while obtaining extraordinary achievements with business and family. A national association can achieve all that. We are living in a time where caution must be taken before there is a total decay of small business, faith, family, friends and community. So, as not to further jeopardize small business, we need to come forward and conform to a commitment. This commitment will assure a better America for retailers in the twenty-first century and beyond.

With a gigantic association such as a National Organization of Retailers as a solid foundation, we can better ourselves and be prepared to elevate our employees, thus making the employee/employer relationships stronger. In turn, we can improve our relationships with the customers who patronize the stores, renewing the spirit of friendliness.

The age of technology has advanced and created the modern day work environment. Therefore, the self-employed members need to advance their own cause. A cause for the future existence of individual proprietorship can be achieved through the N.O.R. in the age of computers. Technology has revolutionized every division of the economy. We must use it.

The Internet is an intrinsic component of the expanding and industrialized nation. We shall make progress using our computers. We can take advantage of modern technology to further our business needs and create a business landscape never before known. Owners of small business with a National Organization of Retailers get ready for the best life you will ever have.

Shakespeare's, *The Tempest V.I. 199*
"LET US NOT BURDEN OUR REMEMBRANCES
WITH A HEAVINESS THAT'S GONE"

Remedy + Repetition = Reward

Entrepreneurs may have been delayed, but hard working retailers cannot be denied. We must create a new environment for the small business sector so our economy can rocket through the 21st century and brighten the third millennium.

National Organization of Retailers

When the Clinton Administration left the White House in 2000, a large surplus of money remained. The next administration quickly diminished the financial overflow, putting the United States in debt many trillion dollars with its delusions of grandeur. All the administration has accomplished by building this debt is the near crash of the American economy.

Late government intervention, little knowledge of the financial burden and not understanding the mismanagement of Savings and Loans, Banks, Brokerage houses, Insurance companies and the auto industries illustrates the inability to stabilize our economy by not acting soon enough before it became a financial hazard.

Many universities should be investigated for they in turn will want bailout money. Who oversees the unbelievably state universities presidents, coaches and administrators paychecks, perks and bonuses while the universities themselves are going deeper in debt? There is no form of normalcy. Overspending is an addiction that needs to be cured.

The first entity, Savings and Loans mortgage foreclosures was responsible for triggering the downward spiral, thus propelling the economy deeper into debt. At present the first bailout taken from the $700 billion emergency fund went to AIG. A couple more bailouts costing billions were in play. Mismanagement gets the prize.

A bailout funding for Wall Street is still no guarantee that the economy will succeed in the future. Research has not been established to what generated this crisis in the first place. Where did company finances go? Is this a situation like Enron where the fat cats misused funds and embezzled large sums of money? Shortly before the fall of AIG the administrators of the company were given $250,000 bonuses. America is off course.

There has clearly been gross misuse of funds over a period of years that needs to be investigated or the four entities will continue to encounter the same financial crises in the coming years.

The bottom line: employers and employees of small businesses will be responsible for covering a large percentage of the bill, while millions of small businesses continue to file for bankruptcy. Where is the government bailout for these companies? Enough is enough and bailout money should be given to small businesses in time of crisis. We must unite.

In conclusion President Bill Clinton's biggest legacy, probably not in his library, was his ability to not spend the surplus while keeping our country in financial growth and international peace.

Secretary of State Hillary Rodham Clinton speaking to an audience in Africa, August, 2009, "I cannot excuse the past and I will not try. We can either think about the past and be imprisoned by it or decide we're going to have a better future and work to make it." Although, it was not directly related to retailers, its perfection was never more eloquently spoken; thus the quotation fits the dilemma of small business leaders.

CHAPTER 22

N.O.R. SITE DEVELOPMENT

After purchasing the land at the four locations, a national building will be erected. Extra land surrounding the construction sites will be leased to retailers interested in the development of the family/business community. The proposed illustration provides all the necessities for wholesome family living in an otherwise business oriented atmosphere. Each facility is essential. Another building of interest constructed and used by the N.O.R. will be the auditorium for lectures and cultural activities. Scheduling activities around conferences will keep the assembly hall occupied. A director and staff would be appointed.

Adjacent to the auditorium is a conveniently located motel and restaurant for out-of-towners and their families in for business conventions, meetings, workshops, etc. Nearby is a recreational playground, with laundry facilities and a cafeteria for a quick bite to eat. For those who favor the intrigue of museums, look no further. Across from the museum are two centers of technology, one for appliances and appliance services, and one for computers and maintenance.

A lavishly green park marks the city square. A sparkling water fountain is prominently displayed in front of the health club and by an automobile service station. In keeping with the health trend, a state of the art medical center is one block over, along with businesses such as a pharmacy, supermarket, law office, post office and a brokerage firm in order to meet the primary needs of the present and up and coming families. Yet another motel and eating establishment are situated nearby for further accommodations of visitors to the community district.

Along this other section of the mall is a gas station and garage-option parking for mall pedestrians. In keeping with the recreational theme is a mini-golf course offering 18 holes of challenging greens and a plethora of artificial waterfalls and mountains canyons as obstacles for whoever wishes to test his or her skills. Further along the line is a hotel/arcade/casino/celebrity entertainment dining room to keep the interest of all ages. The hotel/casino, in particular, will bring in much revenue to the area, with most of it coming from tourists in a manner very similar to that of Las Vegas or Atlantic City, but on a smaller scale. Next to the casino and arcade are two restaurants offering quick and delicious fast food and a coffee shop serving breakfast 24 hours a day.

The top block of the business section is the most diverse. A mini-mall is situated across from the gymnasium. The gym offers a health club, with a body building room, basketball courts, multipurpose rooms and a swimming/diving pool. A bar district is built next to the mini-mall to accommodate the needs of late night socialites and partygoers. In the middle of all the excitement is an outdoor beer garden with many places for people to sit down, walk around and generally enjoy themselves. With this same theme in mind, a restaurant district is located one square block over to cater to those who like to dine out and frequent restaurant environments. Again, an outdoor food garden is located within the square to entertain the restaurant patrons with live music and a place to relax after a delicious and filling meal chosen from a variety of diverse and ethnic offerings along with international cuisines.

As can be seen, something that was not mentioned above is the condo district that outlines one side of the complex. Beyond these structures is a large park with walking paths, many trees and a lake. Another important feature of the district that also was not mentioned because it is its own entity is the parking. Many cities suffer from the woes of traffic congestion and have difficulties remedying the situation. However, what makes this one different is that there is ample parking day and night all over the district to accommodate the large flow of traffic that is present on a daily basis.

Outlying the top block of the business district is a high quality, low cost housing development that epitomizes the ideal of an all-American neighborhood. Located sporadically throughout this section are several selections of places to worship such as a church, synagogue, temple etc. to make attending services more accessible to the citizens of the surrounding areas. This type of living can be summed up in one word, 'rewarding,' because of the diverse array of amenities available to the betterment of the family structure.

Keeping in mind that the city and the residential areas are separate entities of one another, they are still interrelated in various ways. For example, provisions will be made with the nearby city for schooling, ambulance service, hospitals, fire protection, a courthouse, cable, waste disposal, water, burial etc. Urbanizing suburbia: this is the basis of the family business concept. The combining of inner-city luxury with a taste of suburban life will sure enough nurture an environment capable of not only meeting, but also exceeding the needs of people everywhere. This metropolitan resort is the ideal vision of an America in the 21st century.

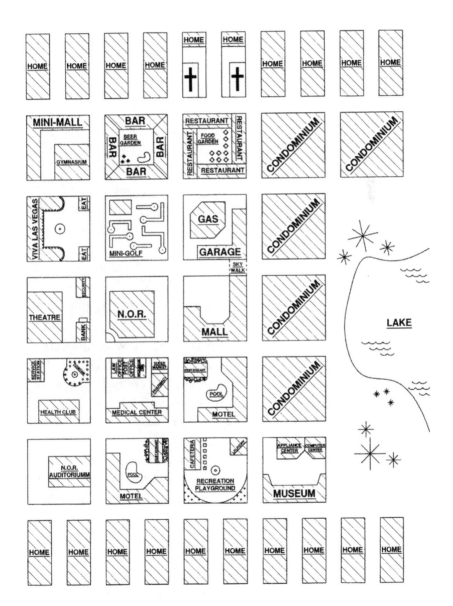

CHAPTER 23

NOW—WHAT?

Innovations in technology and software courtesy of Bill Gates, Steve Jobs, and others, have contributed heavily to our economy's wealth. The United States government is suppressing the advancement of technology by pressing lawsuits on Intel Technology and Microsoft. Justice Department vs. Microsoft—Federal Trade Commission vs. Intel monopolizing this unique industry is one that should not be challenged by the law.

The stock market started on a downward spiral when government interfered with the leaders of computer technology. It was hoped that it would end quickly, but that wasn't to be. It is now felt that when it is finally settled the market recovery might not be forthcoming. Too many people will have lost too much money to consider re-investing into the future market.

Millions of people in the 1990's have reaped the benefits and rewards of this country's escalating economy, and this type of monopoly meets with the approval of 83 percent of the people. Government intervention, again, has caused a recession and whatever else may come of this monopoly issue. Modern technology has moved this country to new levels previously unknown.

The leaders of technology have endowed large income jobs for the immense population and have created large portions of unexpected taxes supporting this great nation. Big corporations such as tobacco and technology companies are getting a taste of what small businesses have been getting for years.

If Microsoft and Intel are misunderstood, then upgraded communications are critical. It is true that the gigantic industries are a challenge for new companies; therefore, federal financial assistance is beneficial. After crushing small business, the American Dream has again been shattered for both the tobacco companies and technology's Microsoft and Intel. Entrepreneurs and technology innovators could not have foreseen this intervention by the bureaucracy.

Big government has drained small business. A word of caution: It is improbable to conceive that you are a victim while in the midst of it. The Senate bill proposed to keep teenagers from smoking—financially penalizing retailers across the country—compares to a scenario in which the person who sold the ski mask to the bank robber is arrested. Duh! A reality check is grossly needed.

Enron, World Com, Tyco etc. have further jeopardized the economy by altering reports and taking all the money for such things as a $6,000 dollar shower curtain, multi vacations, two million dollar birthday parties and exuberant paychecks. The CEOs, leaving 401k shareholders and many other senior citizens who had their money invested in stocks penniless, has lost track of ethics.

In this area of denial, concrete evidence cannot be provided for the following assumptions. The decision is your choice. As Americans we must feel free to speak our beliefs without fear of persecution but with perspicacity.

Face it, Washington is utterly obsessed with explosive government, huge taxes, penniless jobs, starving employers and keeping the American Dream just that a dream. The bureaucracy invents laws which they themselves cannot comply. Denial and unethical decisions jeopardize the **long-term** stability of the economy. These policies must be reprimanded not condoned. With our economy being led by those who practice truth distortions and immoral decision-making, it is no wonder what is really driving down our modern society.

Congress has made it perfectly clear they are anti-small business, technology and marriage by creating more problems for everyone across the country.

To analyze, small business is carrying the burden of charging more tax money for cigarettes and checking everyone's ID.

There is a marriage tax penalty. A married couple pays more than $1,400 dollars in taxes compared to an unmarried couple living together. By the time this book is publisher changes may have occurred.

However, in this book we are concerned about the progress of small business. The above is why an N.O.R. must rely on ethics and a straightforward set-up to strengthen the foundation without repercussions. In no way do we want any of our policies tied up in court.

Without a network of support, one person alone cannot make a difference by today's standards. We must unite especially as voters. Small business is one piece of the economy where a day's hard work may have no financial rewards or benefits. The group being taxed the most, goes without. Is this fair? I'm glad you understand. We go directly to a N.O.R. where families will be personified. We must develop our innovations, remain incisive and get involved together to save the future.

It is of necessitation people who have struggled all their lives be connected to an affluent and better world. Politicians will not do it, never did, never have and never will. They are crushing America's Dreams. The impact of a National Organization of Retailers to gain rewards for ethics, honesty and hard work is long overdue.

There is no other job in this world than a self-made person trying to capture the American Dream. When intervening, government would be most helpful by rewarding and thanking owners of small businesses for their efforts.

Pioneers of Technology: Never have so few done so much for so many—due to the fact that innovators in technology have connected the global world together with computerized gadgets, maybe the likes of Bill Gates and Steve Jobs as political leaders of our country are not far in the future. Innovators could bring technocracy and bureaucracy together. Someone must stop government spending. If anything ever twinkles down, it is the people emulating our government's spending beyond their means.

The leaders of technology in the 1990s have done many things: a.) Connected us; b.) Introduced high paying jobs that made it so more people could work and c.) In turn created a huge amount of tax money; d.) Done more for more family ethics; e.) More people are working out of their homes by way of computerized offices; f.) Everyday innovations—which will start up again once the innovators, get court matters out of the way g.) Technology gave us "toys" that will take a lifetime to acknowledge; h.) Made it less expensive to communicate with our friends across the land; i.) And most of all gave us a sense of worth. God, you've got to love innovators like that. As mentioned before in the latest poll, 83% of the people disapproved of the Justice Department lawsuit to divide Microsoft into two companies. Bill Gates is already an icon in the eyes of the people. He has made life a little easier for many. Bill Gates unselfishly made enormous contributions to charities.

By now, it is apparent how Congress has bastardized small businesses, made a general debauching of F.D.R.'s New Deal and fragmented Corporate America by its many lawsuits.

What Next?

If you are your own commodity such as a movie star, pro athlete, singer, model etc., are you bureaucracy's next target? All independent entrepreneurs need protection and assurance, especially the fine people just mentioned who volunteer their talents by raising money to help others. Isn't this the real focus of life? Living life with all the fundamentals is to be encouraged not discouraged.

One may be king of the world "per se", but if you are not willing to help others, you have nothing. One of the biggest goals of the American Dream is to touch and embrace other lives without mistreating anyone. One of the worst scenarios is for others to have selfish intentions.

Personally, Brad Pitt is the personification of love for everyone. Is he saintly? I think so. With his unselfish desire he has created a dream for victims of hurricane Karina. His inspiration is fair beyond anyone's imagination. By offering his time and money to restore New Orleans is a gift. There is no greater gift than helping others in need.

The principle assets of an individual are love of the family, faith, community and unselfish relationship with others, especially those who are less fortunate. If ethics becomes a distorted blur, then you have nothing. You can fool yourself and be justly rewarded, but your guts are ripped apart. Some may add to their substantial wealth; however, the true meaning of life may have been lost.

The bottom line is perseverance. Rise above those that try to rain on your parade. **While doing what has to be done, stay away from those who say it can't be done.** Every time the government believes you are making more money than they are, Congress for every action will figure out a way to present an equal or opposing government taxpayer financed program.

State governments are sleazy also. In Ohio they lowered sales tax; thus added a community activity tax. At the end of the year businesses must pay a percentage of their profit to the state government. What Sleaze!

One idea for certain is that small business collectiveness is the only way to get where they need to go. The federal government is not in a position to understand the dilemma of the small business owner; thus, making it extremely difficult if not eminently improbable for any independent businessperson to push any business agenda through Congress. Even the rich and famous are not exempt. If we cannot persuade Congress to help small business (loans, no way—we don't need another detriment) and correct the flaws by which our money is being spent, then the people will have to tolerate undesirable legislators along with the unconditional waste of tax money. Congress's lack of compassion toward small business has extended toward some not so big corporations.

In the late 90's there was a government surplus many thanks to computer technology. One can only imagine the amount of surplus there would be without government waste. Ironically, this same technology will indirectly affect almost everyone.

It is virtually predictable as to the direction of taxation the American people are subjected. It is questionable and should be known how Congress is spending each and every penny of the tax money.

If the nation had a national sales tax, the retailers of America could each eliminate weeks wasted doing payroll bookwork. It seems that simple, functional and practical remedies elide our lawmakers. At present, it is not humanly possible for our course of direction to accelerate at the speed in which technology shifts.

As the main metamorphosis, N.O.R. will make a significant impact on the business landscape in the 21st century. Unity can no longer be igNORed. With persistence and continued hard work, the future retailers will achieve their goal of prosperity and family life combined.

A National Organization of Retailers is the only option. We must dedicate ourselves to an association in order to keep the small business landscape alive; thus, perseverance is vital to overcome past misfortune. Desire to change will be the key to survival. This dramatic transformation of individualism with conformity will inspire the future generations of retailers.

Opportunity need not be ostracized. With honest and ethical solutions, N.O.R. will make a noble influence on the determination of our destiny—restoring the real American Dream. It will be fun. Then maybe we can enjoy a humorous side of the business atmosphere.

Through the rapid pace of innovations in computer technology, a National Organization of Retailers will achieve an electrifying furtherance to the perennial top. The N.O.R. site is our remedy for a tightened family/business premise. Integrity, understanding and compassion must be honored by all unless some wish otherwise. Collectively we endure and succeed.

As an actor manipulates the audience to believe in his character, many ideas politicians exploit are untruths, yet, we believe. Fascinating is the way the public is mesmerized only to be disappointed; thus, people go back for more of the same when their politicians are up for reelection. A correction is germane. In time there is a Franklin Delano Roosevelt or Abraham Lincoln somewhere, but can he/she survive the trials and tribulations that have plagued many of today's political leaders? I think so.

In the new economy, mental power—ethics and integrity is equally as vital as physical power—diligence or hard work. However, if the mentality is stepping on others for prosperity, then this power is distorted; consequently, beautiful as everything is, it will eventually collapse. A leader of foresight will **avoid** this pitfall. With a lot of work and faith maybe soon our aspirations will be answered so we can make America new for everyone, again.

A recession/depression economy must be solved permanently to everyone's satisfaction. Today's (2009-2010) financial disaster cannot be solved with archaic solutions used during the thirties' depression. This era is worse than the crash of '29.

Greed, one of the seven deadly sins, is the main culprit. The saddest part is that people's greed has gotten worse as we go into 2011. Once that snowball got rolling, the frozen piece gained a speed unable to stop.

Remedy + Repetition = Reward

Small Business

Our federal legislators don't get it. They are too far removed as to the needs of the people who have small businesses. Someday this will all change if we unite and come together as one people,

The future landscape of small business needs shelter and support in order to stabilize America's economy. Individuals seeking independence in business need support and protection for success.

As the bailout plan for big corporations is unfolding, millions of jobs are lost by small businesses. Many retailers are unable to cope because their expenses are going up while profits are going down. Federal, state and local government demands on small business, filings reports and utility costs are devouring what little profit is made.

In the last couple of years many stores informed the Security Exchange of their closing plans.

A National Organization of Retailers might have saved these entities. Loans do not necessarily generate jobs. Loans incur a debt. In foresight over borrowing could bankrupt a small business. Politicians have no interest in the demise of entrepreneurs.

One doesn't bailout Wall Street to save Main Street. One bails out Main Street while assisting Wall Street. Small stores only hope is an organization. The bottom line, eliminate greed to save capitalism. Start reducing prices across the broad, eliminating exuberant paychecks, bonuses and perks.

Salaries need to be closer together by getting rid of the "fat-cats". Building stores to compete with the Mega stores that carry foreign merchandise, produce the best automobiles to compete with foreign cars by hiring competent employees and hire skilled engineers to create cars with the better precision than foreign cars.

Remedy + Repetition = Reward

CHAPTER 24

MISMANAGEMENT IS REWARDED?

According to President Teddy Roosevelt—which is also manifest in The Constitution—what makes America great is that we have an *obligation* to speak out about our government. This is why we have the First and Second Amendments. Basically, I believe we have a good government. However, they seem to have little interest in owners of small business, make promises they do not fulfill and keep us confused and vulnerable. Perhaps this is a function of the monies big corporate interests pour into political candidates' campaigns, but whatever the case, such a situation, I believe, is simply **not** good. It's extremely uncomfortable to think lawmakers are anti-small business, but using a phrase from the famous football broadcaster, Howard Cosell, "That's the way it is."

To save the longevity of America's small businesses it is necessary for a foundation such as a National Organization of Retailers be developed. When it comes to large corporations failing, the government interferes, for instance, *mismanagement is rewarded*. AIG, banks and the auto industry should be eradicated, not rewarded. The federal government is inadequate and highly unethical.

Congress didn't put conditions on the bailout money. If it had then chances are small business would have gained momentum. Congress seems to have a one track mind and sadly it's in the wrong direction. President Bill Clinton's administration had the ability and acted responsibly with tax money which is quite the opposite of present lawmakers.

Time Magazine's March 30, 2009 cover: "The Bailout Bomb AIG = WMD." No company or individual should be so powerful they can destroy the capitalistic system. Small businesses must provide their own comfort zone. Large corporations rewarded for their greed, along with Congress' inability to allocate money with no restrictions, is like a guided missile gone astray.

As mentioned before, Jim Cramer, the stock market guru on television's "Mad Money" says of our leaders, "They know nothing." While bailing out the fat cats government fails to respond to the necessities of small business. <u>This in itself is sufficient reason for entrepreneurs to unite.</u> Why are we waiting? We all had a lot of hope in the new administration, but it isn't to be.

Nothing is too big to fail or too small to succeed. Rewarding mismanagement is damaging the very fabric of American aspirations. We all suffer bad economic news. Tolerating irresponsible leadership, corporations find themselves on the road to bankruptcy; thus, government intervention issuing bailout money to save failures keeps America on the wrong track.

Small businesses closing throughout the country in the last two years eliminated millions of workers. Still there are many more jobs uncertain. To overcome this, we must unite. The government's perspective of business owners will not change until we come together to form an association. Most small businesses opening today are defenseless. An association provides the necessary support allowing entrepreneurs to reach their full potential.

Once united, help from the government will not be imminent. That would be a blessing. Corporate greed isn't the agenda; thus, the federal administration may become a larger detriment by association. Small-business owners need not be afraid of the political system or drawn into its notorious ways.

If Congress hadn't interfered with large, failing, unneeded and mismanaged banks, then properly managed community banks with strong ethics, hard work, trust and ability would have prospered astronomically fulfilling part of their American Dream.

Due to the insult the integrity of private enterprise is jeopardized. In 2009, one hundred and forty banks and collectively their many branches had shut down with over four hundred banks to follow. By

September of 2010, another one hundred and eighteen banks had failed. A total of two hundred and fifty eight small banks have collapsed.

One gets the impression that the government is repressing the hard workers of this country. How could Congress possibly put small banks out of business? But they did. Bailouts for the rich and greedy were uncalled for and extremely detrimental to those less fortunate. Even if the bailout saved the country, it was wrong. There was a right way to save this nation, but Congress is incapable of making right decisions especially ones that involve owners of small business.

The bullies are in the big banks, and the nice people work in community banks. Judging by my experience, I ask a bank that received bailout money to not honor anyone trying to withdraw money from the business account electronically. Response was they could not do it. When asking the community bank the same question, the response was, "No problem".

One cannot help but wonder if this administration is further bankrupting the economy. Bailouts costing millions of people their jobs, astronomical college costs, not giving Social Security recipients their cost of living increase and mortgages among a few, illustrate how many individuals will be in debt the rest of their life.

What is America's obsession with over-spending? Credit is probably one of the major factors in this country's downfall. In good faith maybe some people cannot pay their bills due to job loss. In retrospect maybe a lot of people have the money, but use funds for luxuries instead of paying off debts. This needs to change to sustain our economy.

However, the bailout helped plunge the economy into a swirling, unstoppable recession/depression. It was after the bailout that many jobs were eliminated and many more job losses are yet to come in the small business private sector. Two years ago, and even today jobs created would have stopped any nation's downward spiral. Bailout was a flat-out failure and helped cause a costly and devastating recession/depression.

There is no concrete evident as to what the economy would be like without a bailout and jobs not being shipped overseas. Small business could not be any worse off than they are right now. We have only the administration's perspective which only implies we would be worse off. Two years and we still do not know for sure how it will play out. Shipping jobs overseas was a no-no.

Where did our foresight go? Things are so bad that when a man informed me he had just lost his job and his son was starting college, tears were hard to hold back. It's **not** a pretty picture.

When it comes to debts of any kind, reality doesn't set in until the payment comes due. Then it's too late. It's heartbreaking when debts pile up and a job is lost. Debts that are paid late add interest and penalties creating a bigger debt responsibility.

To their credit, unironically, at least Congress 1) passed the (credit) Bill of Rights to help protect individuals and small businesses from predatory lending policies of big banks and 2) the fed. proposed limits to bank card merchant fees. We'll have to see how these issues play out. However, it is a couple of steps in the right direction for small businesses.

Colonial Bank, with its 346 branches in the south was seized by the government and saw many people lose their jobs. When banks collapse, their rivals buy its branches, deposits and most of the assets. The fat cats create money stockpiles for bailout banks.

When small banks continue to shut down, customers are forced to put their money in bailout banks; thus, creating a good financial stock market investment for the bulls. It's a vicious cycle that has to be broken.

Yet, banks too big to fail according to our government are accepting bailout money from taxpayers for <u>bonuses</u>. Our economy's deficit in the tens of trillions of dollars is concrete proof of mismanaged funds. Expenses, salaries, perquisites and bonuses obviously need to be less than a company's profit for success. **We all know that. Don't we?**

It's an enigma as to how CEOs, CFOs and executives are paid with money the company hasn't earned under their supervision. Replacement is the only way to address the problem. Small business again gets the short end of the stick.

Not all managers are the same, though; the CEO at Hewett Packard made billions for the company before he left in 2010. He earned and deserved every penny of his paycheck. There are some CEOs, CFOs and executives that helped make their companies financially successful.

Listed are a few CEOs that earned their rewards by keeping their corporations profitable and financially secure: Jeff Boyd (PCLN); Dan Amos (AFL); Steve Jobs (AAPL); Jeffrey Bezos (AMZN) and many more successful CEOs, CFOs and executives in 2010. The list is too numerous to mention all.

However, both political parties are using taxpayer's money to reward the undeserving. There are people starving—literally. Again, greed has replaced all values. It's a travesty. Future generations will not have the opportunities of our generation. Not at this rate, anyway.

Owners of small business cannot relate to this type of environment. To keep their businesses operating many proprietors will work all day with no financial rewards. The families go without and may be forced to cut back on meals when businesses suffer.

Public universities operate basically the same as bad corporations putting higher education in jeopardy. "Fat cats" heavily rewarded by the taxpayer's money and ample tuition as the universities go deeper in debt. Overspending is unhealthy. As greed enters our educational system, capitalism will soon vanish.

Universities complain that high school graduates are unprepared for college; thus, the same seems true that many executives are unprepared for operating large corporations. One has to wonder where CEOs, CFOs and other executives of failure got their degrees.

The same executives bankrupting Bear Stearns and Goldman Sachs were hired to bankrupt the economy. And what a good job they've done. Successful executives seem to be overlooked.

Economic growth for entrepreneurs has been stopped with no financial reform in sight. Small businesses need customers. In 2010 and 2011 Social Security recipients did not receive a cost of living raise; consequently, their spending in 2010 and 2011 will be the same as 2009.

The recipients will be two years behind in the cost of living, and there is no compensation in sight. Congress (Robin Hood in reverse) is stealing from the poor and giving to the rich.

The frustrating reality is if the cost of living would increase a Social Security retiree's paycheck by $100 a month in 2010, the receiver will lose $1,200 in that year alone. Again in 2011 if the cost of living would increase the receiver's paycheck by $100 a month now the loss of not only $2,400 but $3,600 plus the cost of living times the $100 a month from the year before would also be added to the loss. This loss will continue to grow the rest of their years. Imagine how much money would be lost if there is no increase in cost of living for Social Security recipients in 2012. If the government doesn't give a cost of living raise in 2012, it will be devastating.

A proposal of a stimulus package for $250 for Social Security recipients was voted down in March, 2010 by the senate 50—47. Yet, the Senate as well as all federal employees got raises in January 2010. It is nothing short of hilarious to think these candidates were voted into office to help the people. Congress has marked themselves as a detriment to Social Security recipients, usually to the benefit of large corporations that donate to candidates' campaigns.

One bad apple spoils the whole bunch. In the case of our leaders we got a majority of bad apples. Everyone who voted against the cost of living raise for our elders must be remembered by the voters in the coming elections.

Most government leaders feel they deserve all the benefits with their jobs, but do not feel that Social Security recipients should get a cost of living increase. What did the administration do with the money paid into Social Security by the recipients? However, when Congress fails to act in the country's' best interest any reward, perqs. or bonuses are simply wrong.

Individual Social Security recipients are the only ones that should be collecting money promised them. To use the funds for any other reason is simply unjust. No one has a right to rob this cookie jar. The dynamics set up by President FDR. are nothing less than perfect. Why must our leaders ruin the lives of older citizens?

Congress gets Social Security while not paying into the system; thus, stealing from the elderly. Most owners of small businesses rarely get perks, bonuses and what is really deserved through no fault of their own. Yet, Congress gets what they deserve. The self-employed and their employees deserve their Social Security and the cost of living raise every year.

Our leaders are shutting down our economy. Jobs have been forced out of the country, spending power limited, the percentage of jobs lost each month is devastating and the elderly are suffering. Yet, the rich, who hoard their money, got tax breaks renewed; consequently, Congress is supporting less spending. Lawmakers again display their ignorance for what is good for small business and provide financial safety for the whole economy.

Loans are not the answer for most owners of small business. Many establishments are struggling financially; thus, entrepreneurs cannot afford another debt. Businesses need spenders. Location, location, location becomes **location/spending, location/spending, location/spending.** The government lacks the remedies. What does one expect when there is <u>greed?</u>

However, due to the lack of business sales, its obvious customers have no money to spend. Many businesses have lost a great deal of profit, and loans will be needed much to their dismay.

Loans are necessary for equipment, stock and utilities. If people don't spend, then another debt may be disastrous to the owner. Congress is no help to small business in this regard.

Jobs must be created. Again, America would not have this problem if there wasn't a bailout and jobs shipped overseas. President John Kennedy had the foresight of a coming recession/depression and saved America by creating the answers before the problems developed; therefore, he was an intelligent man of foresight and solutions. Be assured he would have given receivers of Social Security their cost of living raise.

Our present legislators, on the other hand, demonstrate very little business acumen. To increase spending it's necessary to lower payroll taxes, no taxes for workers who make less than $25,000 and give recipients of Social Security their cost of living increase <u>going back to January 2010</u> (no increase in Social Security checks reduced spending by billions of dollars). Many people use their retirement money for food. It's shameful! Let me repeat: many elders spend their Social Security retirement money for food, not luxuries. They live at a barely livable wage.

Our government does not understand that Social Security was put aside for elderly people to better their lives in later days. It wasn't supposed to make anyone rich, but it also wasn't meant to make anyone poor. People entitled to the insurance money paid their dues. This really shuts down our economy big time.

The Feds are incapable of putting the country back on track by messing around with elder's retirement money. They are saying one thing and doing another. People that believe anything stated by politicians are gullible. I honestly get sick taking Social Security and Medicare from my employee's paycheck. I get sicker knowing these culprits, the federal economists, are stealing worker's hard earned money. No employer should feel that way.

If the government would use their energy solving problems instead of personifying them, the country would be better off. Congress with their imperfections knows what the flaws are in Social Security, but are incapable to emend them.

Americans need a strong administration composed of compassion not greed. An administration giving back the money lost the two years mentioned to Social Security recipients, because that is the only way recipients will be able to deal with rising prices in the future.

Baby-Boomers' rumors are a myth. They all paid into Social Security. So why wouldn't the money be in place? If the money isn't at the Social Security office, then where is it? Baby-Boomers paid their dues.

Many owners of small business are forced to deplete their savings in order to keep their bankrupt establishments operating. Living on past income is a difficult way to live. Many work long hours every day hoping their businesses will turn around and make a profit large enough to support the family needs. The objective is a solution to get back on the right track to reach our destination.

The "fat cats"—managers and administrators—somehow manage to get raises regardless of the failings of their country, universities or corporations they represent. Small business cannot operate under these conditions. It doesn't work.

According to USA Today, the newspaper, March 5-7 issue: "Feds outpace private workers by $7,000." average salary $67,691. "These salaries do not include the value of health, pensions and other benefits, which averaged $40,785 per federal employee in 2008 vs. $9,882 per private worker, according to the Bureau of Economic Analysis." While small business suffers, the government employees have fulfilled their dream with taxpayer's money".

However, government jobs outpace private enterprise. They get raises yearly, often regardless of the economy's status; however, federal employees are facing a pay freeze in the next few years starting in 2011. Almost six billion dollars yearly will not be spent due to a freeze.

With limitations on Social Security recipients' paychecks and a freeze on federal employees pay raises, small businesses as usual will suffer the most. Less spending will be in the double digit billions leaving small businesses in the lurch—less sales, less profit.

Something is not right. It's hard to work all day just to put food on the table. Our leaders will not contribute in any way to help small business achieve their American Dream. The present administration and past administrations are and have been anti-small business. Although Congress says otherwise, there is no reason to believe otherwise. In a take/take situation, something has to change for small business to move forward.

Meanwhile, it's not unusual to see businesspeople buying toiletries at the market, yet federal or state administrators do not buy or pay out of their salaries for idiosyncrasies or personal trips on company, university or corporation planes. In most cases it would be advisable to fly commercial paying their own way.

Small business success can be achieved through the power of a dream. To make that dream a reality it involves hard work (mentally and physically), honesty, ethics, integrity and above all a commitment to one another by uniting. Entrepreneurs must organize and work together for future progress of that dream.

America is resilient I've always heard. Does this mean we are not resilient enough to overcome the bankruptcy of businesses bigger than America? I think not.

Legislature's inability to solve problems is understandable when greed becomes their top priority. They must be of the conviction that eliminating greed supplies them with the knowledge to solve; therefore, it's understandable why legislators lack the ability to remedy problems.

Political influence, issuing more wealth to societies' failures, has created a larger nightmare for small business and is keeping the country on the wrong track without justification. Oh, sure we would be in worse shape without a bailout. Who started that myth?

Anyone with intelligence saw this recession/depression coming fifteen years ago. I've always assumed the CEOs, CFOs and executives would be retired enjoying their millions by now. That wasn't to be. These culprits were holding out for a bigger lottery. In 2010 and 2011 with trouble brewing there is a mass departure.

Next will be a university top echelon exodus. Their cup is also sated. Congress again will be asked for a bailout while the taxpayer and students are left the financial burden. How do you refuse education?

With regular inspections universities' financial failure can be avoided. A superior audit would be good for starters. Universities' administrators are also taken by greed. Again, they continue getting raises, while staff cuts and faculty furloughs are becoming the norm—not to mention that staff and faculty, those who actually make the schools run, have often seen no raises in recent years.

We are interested in small business uniting for all the right reasons. Guided by ethics, unselfish entrepreneurs would have the capability to remedy any situation regardless of its level.

Our lawmakers have made it harder for small businesses to succeed. There isn't much time to correct their dislike toward independent entrepreneurs.

In my many years of business, and my father's business years before me, I've seen nothing good come from our legislators concerning the welfare of small business except for President Roosevelt's Social Security plan, and President Kennedy's reduction of income tax. Both Presidents were helpful to everyone.

We can no longer endure legislators' intentions of destroying our businesses or "The American Dream". Through it all, merchants will survive.

Together we are strong. We are trying to make an honest living for our families to have the necessities of life. America needs level minded people to support its future and correct its past. The government is throwing our tax money in the wrong direction.

If $700 billion dollars were given to new, competent and confident leadership, then opening new businesses would move the country in an upward direction. Owners of small shops need to create a level that bailouts given to mismanagement could never achieve. Who ever heard of building structures from the top down? Therefore, the country would be better off without bailouts. And this isn't your everyday propaganda. We've all seen a financially bad two years.

Big businesses and their leaders lacking in productive skills are demoted, not rewarded. The American Dream was shattered once the bailout began.

Rewards belong to the well managed institutions which many have gone bankrupt because of the bailout. Congress says we would be better off bailing out high risk operations. I ask, "In what way?" We would have been saved from a recession/depression if there wasn't a bailout for the undeserving rich.

A recession/depression that started several years ago could have been averted if jobs were created not lost. Yet, two years later people are still being laid off with no end in sight. Small business needs assistance. **Unification of businesspeople is probably the only way to get the economy back on the right track.** Employers have been repressed far too long. Entrepreneurs need their own form of government.

Federal government is not the only one to over-tax and over-regulate small business. Local and state governments also stifle small business. Some tax money is used to increase their federal, state and local paychecks while devouring self-employed profit. Small businesses can't afford their governmental habits. What is being said, the cost of living goes up while the entrepreneur's profit goes down.

Owners of small business have the capabilities of reversing an unnecessary demon. Government's market psychology is incorrect. Money could better be spent on health care, older citizens, **Social Security, Medicare**, (which government is doing their best to bankrupt—both SS & Med.), jobs and the necessities of life that need improvement.

In small business today it is sink or swim with no life jackets, no boats to pick you up and with little assistance. United is almost mandatory. It's the support to keep the owners of small enterprise afloat.

Given a bailout, propaganda seems to be the name of the game. When small businesses collapse new stores are established. We were told all three car companies would go bankrupt. If one car company goes belly up, there is no reason not to believe the other two car companies would boom. All jobs would be saved and only the voracious, executive culprits would be removed.

According to the Labor Department, small businesses are lagging in the recovery. What recovery? 61.8% jobs cut with only 54.1% created in 2009. There's no recovery. There are more people in a depression than those in the recession. When the recession is over and inflation sets in, there will be many more people in a depression.

Percentage-wise we are losing more jobs now than ever before. If your company has eight employees and five were laid off, then there are only three left. It's the analogy we explained in Chapter Five about the steaks. Sure there are fewer jobs lost today than two years ago, but the percentage is higher.

Companies and corporations should be held to the same responsibilities as small businesses. There is no logical reason for bailouts. There are many millionaires available to start up new industries. If we do not correct our economy, many more people will be without food.

How focused are we on our other priorities. Help eludes us when it comes to our senior citizens, orphans, homeless, jobless etc. However, we provide aid to foreign countries, yet, our own don't have food, shelter or medical help. What is the master plan? The churches and less fortunate people do their share by providing pantries collecting food for those in need. Yet, there is no indication our present administration is providing for the poor. Our greed keeps us on the wrong road to prosperity.

Just who are the greedy? Is it the politicians, the executives of failing corporations who drained their companies financial resources or is it a combination of both? Regardless, many employers and employees are losing their jobs for their well managed operations. Small business needs better options. Good shouldn't be punished while the rich are rewarded.

While the path our government has chosen does not parallel with the ideas explained in this book, the concepts offer valid solutions for an ethical businessperson. Our motto: ***Remedy + Repetition = Reward*** is on the right track.

America wants big. A small business association with its enormous membership would be a revolution involving millions. With this in mind, we will go from nowhere to the top of government's priority list. However, proprietorship economics from an organization made up of self employed individuals may be able to distance small business from the legislators trying to bankrupt our establishments.

One only need look at our bar owners that have lost their position in life because of a law banning smoking in establishments. Many have earned an honest living while the government eliminated their business operations by their harmful ways. Maybe there are some people that don't want to smoke where they drink. That's okay. But leave the ones alone who want a smoke and drink bar.

Forcing people to smoke on the street in freezing cold weather has put their health in jeopardy. No one wants to catch pneumonia. A law such as that has been written and implemented by leaders with no compassion.

Food and Drug Administration pulled another blunder. Safe guarding fire proof cigarettes with ingredients leaving the smokers with illnesses never before known and has put smoker's health in genuine danger.

Small business cannot put up with the shenanigans of government's dysfunctional Ethics House Committee, impaired Small Business Administration and now an abnormal Food and Drug Administration. We need our own form of a good administration that cares for small business and humanity.

When developing an NOR there is no way we can function in the same manner as the above mentioned. We've got to work hard in order to be practical, ethical, promising and eternal.

Back to the future

Putting a huge tax on tobacco products bringing in billions of the taxpayer's money starting April 1, 2009 proves the new government is not walking the talk. Will smokers butt out? What happened to the "No new taxes?" Didn't we go through this with the 1988 administration? History repeats itself. The poor and whatever is left of the middle class picks up the tab.

Look out small business. If the government put a new tax on cigarettes after a month in office, they are going to tax the middle class anyway they can. Worst yet some taxes we won't even understand for lack of knowledge; however, we will feel the burden. Again, politicians say one thing to get elected and do just the opposite once in office. Their lack of conviction deprives small businesses ethical way of operation.

Pardon stupidity. Members of both parties depend on untruths to get elected. Maybe the two parties should unite: therefore, congressional members would be more likely to vote for the issues instead of siding with a certain party. Sidestepping accomplishments by not matching their rhetoric is nothing more than a handful of bursting bubbles.

More importantly government is following the countries that were destroyed by greed. **Acquisitiveness must stop**. <u>Any country relying on greed has not survived throughout history</u>.

According to First Lady Eleanor Roosevelt as mentioned earlier in this book excessive desire was the downfall of Phoenicia, Carthage, Greece, Rome and Spain. Who says this country is different? Entrepreneurs uniting will not only save small business, but rescue the country from doom.

Health Reform: we've been hustled again. The cost of this entity has been passed on to small businesses. It's time to emulate actor Peter Finch in the movie, "Network" when he says, "We're not taking it anymore."

The government's sleazy way of giving us another debt is preposterous. Just because our government has a spending addiction, doesn't mean we should go deeper in debt. Get thy to a **Spending Addiction Rehab**.

Our government believes failing large corporations should be rewarded. No sense can be made of it. We've got to turn the corner so that small business is treated fairly. Something needs corrected. Spending is an addiction of our government being passed down to the credit card addiction creating debt for everyone.

If small businesses do not negotiate, then a new American Dream will emerge. Maybe it has already. Citizens would be working for the government and renting a house while giving up self-employment and home ownership. However, when the housing bubble burst, family life felt the pain.

Families have left their homes behind for apartment living. No more porch swings, gardens, cookouts or private pools with its outside music. Best of all, there are no mortgages, property taxes or house insurance to pay.

In many cases, Americans move to where their jobs take them. A travel exodus has emerged. Small businesses usually stay the course not having to relocate to a different state; thus, family life can still exist for entrepreneurs.

Realizing the country is moving in the wrong direction could be why some top Congress members decided to leave the political arena.

Congress will have a hard time finding the likes of Evan Bayh. At a news conference in February 2010, Senator Bayh said, "to put it into words I think most people can understand: I love working for the people of Indiana. I love helping our citizens make the most of their lives, but I do not love Congress". Concrete proof one cannot make a difference. A great statesman fighting for the people is rare.

It takes a network of people with the right decisions and an unselfish love for all the people, poor or rich, the family and the business to turn the country around. As mentioned in the last chapter and worth repeating. It will not turn around for any of us until it turns around for all of us.

The unification of entrepreneurs throughout this country can do that with ethics as its foundation. No place for selfishness as well as greed will enter into an organization of self employed. We will be concerned about the welfare of everyone having his or her own business.

It's hard to see our country's best throw in the towel. Realizing this country is on the wrong track could be why Congress's Christopher Dodd and Patrick Kennedy decided to leave the political arena. Sadder yet, great people of this country do not consider running for office. They have their priorities straight not to be overtaken by greed. Their focus is on what is good for all.

There is something to be learned. Family love is the most important thing in the world. Small enterprise coming together is probably the only entity that can save the nation's freedoms, its independence, self reliance, family values and ruination from outside forces such as the seven deadly sins. Decisions must be made as to what the people of this great nation want the American Dream to represent. Avarice is not the answer.

Voters are dissatisfied with Washington partisanship, high unemployment, federal deficit and bonuses for executive failures. It doesn't get any better. Greed has taken over America, and someone has to send the right message to reverse the wrong direction.

Solutions by Congress must be put into play if they want to help the nation and small business move forward: (1) Stamp out greed; (2) job creation; (3) no further bailouts; (4) no sneaky taxes; (5) stop dipping into social security; (6) give cost of living raises to Social Security recipients every year; (7)) leaders not paying into Social Security are not entitled to collect; (8) a 2%-4% Social Security tax on people making over $106,800 for Social Security purposes only; (9) correct present entitlements before starting new ones; (10) stop endangering small business; (11) downsize government; (12) unite bicameral government;

(13) honor promises; (14) and a third party might be phenomenal. We need a change for the better—a change that includes the good life for everyone as promised every four years, but never becomes a reality. Positive change is built on ethics and truths. Rhetoric proclaiming false promises is unnecessary.

We have to organize to save small business from the clutches of fat cats. <u>Social Security recipients robbed</u>. Unethical opportunities by our leaders have jeopardized our nation's retirement system.

Money paid from the payroll into Social Security deprived many employees of food and other necessities of life while they were in the work force. If our employees are not guaranteed support in their later years by the country's retirement program, then employers have no right taking money out of their employees' paychecks

If employees do not get their Social Security and Medicare benefits, <u>then employers are guilty of theft.</u> Therefore we are all victims indirectly of a dysfunctional government through no fault of our own. We've got to make it right.

Our leaders have crippled the process, and should have taken care of Social Security years ago. Meanwhile it is our responsibility by uniting and setting up our own retirement until Social Security is assured.

After being in business a short time my heart took a different direction and that was one of satisfaction. It was important that my employees enjoyed their work. Customer satisfaction was priority number one. It was necessary to please our customers; thus, our profits became secondary.

Small business not only owes it to the self employed of America, but to the country. N.O.R. is the light that can brighten an otherwise dull penniless poor and middle class economy. It is our obligation to restore the American Dream as our forefathers intended with honor, ethics, integrity and support for one another giving us faith, hope, charity and love.

Due to many added taxes and forms to fill out many small businesses cannot survive. The government has their hands in everyone's pocket. The whole country is going bankrupt if the present conditions continue in this deep depression of the poor and middle classes.

America got it wrong. Priorities are out of perspective. Mismanagement + Thief = Reward created a sudden catastrophe. Our motto: **Remedy + Repetition = Reward** defines America.

In hindsight going back to the future, much like the 1950s and 1960s meaning lower prices and lower paychecks would have moved the economy forward. Our perception more and big is better was the downfall. Greed instead of capitalism became the goal.

Part of China's successful economy in the late 20th Century and the first decade of the 21st Century were due to the failure of the United States' ability to compete. Our country failed to emulate China's economy. Our movement was greed; therefore, we increased almost everything across the board thinking that more was better. No lesson has been learned and inflation is on the rise.

If America stays on the wrong track, China will overtake us within the next five to ten years as the world's number one economy. We've got to operate the way we operated in the '50s and '60's low income and low prices. But can America handle that? We could but we won't.

Once on the wrong track in every way then nothing can be accomplished. The knowledge and experience of leaders in small business united can handle anything with the right motivation and ethics.

By Congress' idiotic notions we permitted mega stores with foreign products overshadow our own economy's growth. No remedies were ever attempted. It was then time to go back to the future. But we didn't.

In foresight the country could do that now. In the sixties people made less than a dollar an hour with huge purchasing power. Today to equal the purchasing power of that era an individual must make between twenty-five to thirty dollars an hour. Prices up across the board have never made sense.

Back to the future for success can be a goal if greed is eliminated, and lowered taxes were implemented as in the sixties to stop a downward spiral into an overall depression. It's a challenge.

Remedy + Repetition = Reward

Politicians, although doing the best they can, do not understand or are not knowledgeable of small business responsibilities. Is what they're doing to small business on purpose or is it because they don't understand its negative impact on small business? Politicians are out to get the vote, and whatever the cost they are willing to pay the price. Big business too often foots the bill.

Congress will not protect the backbone of the American economy until we unite. Owners of small businesses coming together could help politicians make right decisions for the good of not only the entrepreneur but for the country.

We have escaped our leader's attention because we failed as individuals and not a group. We are one in number. By not uniting we remain unattached and have only ourselves to rely on. Yet, other groups are in vast numbers. Congress members need allies.

These groups have voting power. We are overlooked because we only have the authority of a single vote which doesn't mean much. In order to stabilize our profession we must organize. Lobbyists can do wonders for the business landscape. It's important to get along with each other so that growth can begin.

Transformation would be humongous. At present, whenever, speaking of merchants a congressperson almost always refers to one isolated incident. They have no clue as to the trials and tribulations of each small shop owner. All will change once merchants unite. Together we can build a new amazing culture helping entrepreneurs create and develop dreams that seemed inconceivable

N.O.R. with its potency in numbers can change the landscape of the American economy. We have to surface as a group. It is the responsibility of entrepreneurs to take small business where it needs to go not where our structure, the American Dream, has fallen.

Any dependence on Congress is a big mistake. Washington doesn't understand the working of small business. Our economy needs businesspeople not stupid leaders that have put the nation's stability at risk. Our economy needs more **spending** in order for job creation. Is anyone listening? I don't think so. It's all about small business working in a dubious and shrinking economy. There is no permanent help in sight for small business.

If there is an offer to shop owners from our administration, extreme caution would be imperative. Motivation would have to be analyzed before an acceptance. Even though some legislators owned small businesses, they illustrate no knowledge to its needs.

Congress is incapable of helping entrepreneurs. Bailouts crippled small businesses causing many to fail especially small community banks and their branches. Government igNORing small business in all the years our "Mom and Pop" were pursuing the American Dream, has been unwise.

In the long run it would be absolutely awesome if we could get rid of government intervention. They've never gotten anything right. The bottom line is: why would owners of small business think Congress could do anything right for them? The ultimate path to prosperity is an N.O.R.

First and foremost greed or super capitalism, whatever one wants to call it, must be eradicated. A National Organization of Retailers advocating capitalism is the magic formula for the longevity of entrepreneurs. The country needs help.

Self-employed individuals and their employees are one of the main sources that can put the United States back on the right track.

Alliances have made this country strong. It's our obligation as working people of America to move our country forward. Charismatic entrepreneurs have been repressed due to separation instead as a group. The struggle to survive for the self-employed is difficult. A network of support is inevitable for future success.

The potential of small business will never be known until an association materializes. At present there is 17% unemployed not 9.6% as reported. There are 7.4% jobless people who are no longer collecting unemployment checks; thus they are not in the equation. Many full-time workers are now working part-time at a reduction across the board. Meanwhile, according to the Department of Labor 136,000 in 2010 and 70,000 in 2009 *government jobs* were created. Wow.

Have you seen the lines at the food pantries? Soup lines in the last depression are nothing compared to those seeking nourishment at food pantries. Hopefully, these people have access to kitchens where they can prepare food.

Many unemployed were working at low paying jobs to purchase food and shelter. Barely meeting needs with what little income they earned.

Coming to the conclusion for owners of small businesses, the reality is:

<u>Only small business can help small business.</u>

OBSERVATION

At the onset of this writing, it was meant to assist people interested in achieving the American Dream. The solution is an association with a labor established for retailers. Entrepreneurs are starving for nourishment, commitment and are in dire need of leadership built on integrity, truths and ethics. The potential growth of people in small business is limited. With an umbrella of protection we can go singing in the rain without raindrops falling on our heads.

In the last decade of the 20th century the country was experiencing "good times". However, sound the economy, there were many small businesses that did not share the experience. Increased expenses and governmental interference have challenged the struggle for survival at the present level. Longer hours at work and less time with the family have put home life at risk.

Eleven years into the 21st century nothing positive has changed to stabilize owners of business. Our tax money is the foundation for federal, state and local governments whose paychecks and perqs. hit the ceiling every year. The American dream is more distorted than it has ever been. Self-employed expenses keep growing; profits are going down, hard work has become harder, the hours are unreal and no federal financial assistant in sight. Family life is practically non existence.

Family orientation within the association is exigent to bring the business and family life back together. Providing outlets by having others care for the children is not sufficient. It is a matter of unconditional love and support for the children that can only be fulfilled with the intensity of their mother and father. Balancing is essential. A happy healthy home life will develop if a parent is available to provide daily sit down meals. The rest of the evening could be enjoyed by the whole family with intimate discussions, humor, recreational activities, working on computers or watching television. When it comes to family, quality time is twenty-four hours a day. Time with the family will be the most cherished days of your life.

Therefore it becomes necessary to create an environment where the whole family can experience and enjoy the true benefits of the interwoven business/ family life.

Four national organizational structures for executive meetings modeled with families in mind are the most vital criteria of the National Organizations of Retailers. This remedy will do something about the unfortunate present family/business circumstances.

It is clear that the present conditions confronting small business must no longer prevail in the 21st century. Less bureaucracy, increased opportunity, positive encouragement and inclusion in the governmental process are of immeasurable importance. With a National Organization of Retailers in place, Congress's perspective of the business landscape will call for some invigorating new strategy.

Many people are entrapped by their tangible possessions. Do not be misled by anyone who has misplaced their priorities and sense of values. The concentration must be first and foremost with our family for love, support and fewer hours spent working the business. Ownership is prioritized only when needed for family necessities not luxuries.

Apparently, what has caused the downward spiral of small business can be attributed to owners of small business for not organizing. The adjustment of the present and future businesses can be accredited to retailers if the necessary steps are taken to develop an association. As composed unflappable individuals, we have the capacity to bring the American Dream back to the reality it once was. We have given all without compensation. The remedy has been set forth in The Case for Small Business to make America a better America for all workers and their families across this nation. We can now "take this job and love it".